The
Magic of Nature

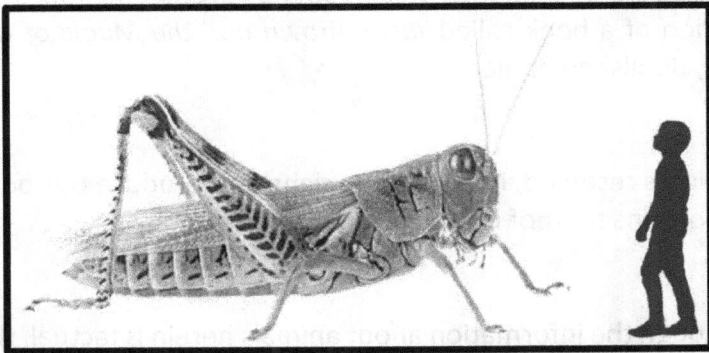

Henry R. Hermann

The beginning of a series of children's books that delve into differences and similarities among animal and plant forms and their environments. This book is a second and improved version of a book called *Jason Brown and the Magic of Nature*, published earlier.

Acknowledgements

It has been my pleasure to work with teachers at all levels of education while at the University of Georgia. It was there that I headed a committee to maintain a connection with schools in and around Athens, Georgia, and it was during this period that I became dedicated to helping young students and their teachers.

When one considers who influences young minds the most, we would have to list teachers of pre-college students at the very top of our list. They not only prepare young students for life in difficult times, but they stimulate the minds of many to consider going on to higher forms of education, e.g., college, graduate school and post graduate studies. I stand in awe of the difficult tasks they sometimes face and their dedication to their teaching responsibilities.

I would like to especially thank Diane Blozis, 5th grade teacher in Ft. Myers, Florida, for using *The Magic of Nature* in her classes. I am indebted to her for her kindness and feedback from her students.

I would also like to thank Mike Wharton and other staff members at Sandy Creek Nature Center in Athens, Georgia, where I was a member of the Board of Directors and had the opportunity of working with children of all ages. Mike and his staff are very special people who always have childrens' interest in mind. Working in that capacity helped me to recognize a genuine interest in Nature by almost all young people. It pointed out to me the importance of explaining the significance of Nature to them in their early years because many people lose sight of the importance of nature as they get older.

It was this sincere interest by young students that prepared me for writing this book, a story about a fifth-grade student who had an overwhelming interest in learning about Nature.

Dedication

To Bradford and Alessandra

It is my hope that this book will stimulate young students to both enjoy Nature and realize the benefits of reading. Both can open up a world of pleasure that often escapes the minds of people growing up in an intense electronically-oriented society.

Preface

Based on thirty years of experience in working with teachers and students of all ages and levels of education, it has been my experience that most young children have a natural interest in science and nature. It is between their childhood years and their early teens that they often lose this natural attraction for science and subsequently learn to ignore the importance of nature and the environment.

This statement is partially based on countless hours of discussion and brain-storming sessions with colleagues, all of which have been education professionals. It is also based on discussions with practicing teachers and experimentation by graduate students that had addressed this problem in their master's and doctoral research. What this means is that if children are not exposed to Nature in their young years, they may never be exposed to it.

While there has been much written about our environment in recent years for readers of all ages, it was during these meetings with other education professionals (throughout the 1980s and early 1990s) that we collectively determined that one of the major causes of this loss of interest was a shortage of stimulating material for students to read to help them think about and appreciate their biological world. In addition, we realized it was a nation-wide phenomenon. This information influenced my direction of teaching throughout my 30-year tenure at the University of Georgia.

As a Professor in the Division of Biological Sciences at the University of Georgia, Lecturer in the Department of Science Education, Science Fair Coordinator and Judge, I maintained an interest in working with teachers and young people and enjoyed bridging the gap between them and science. It was for this reason that I developed several courses for teachers and co-authored a book called *Classroom Activities with Insects* for them to convey information about science to their students. I also developed and taught courses directed at non-science college majors to bring science to individuals who were not science-oriented.

As chairman of a community-oriented committee at the University of Georgia, I had an opportunity to offer seminars for young people of all ages.

Their genuine thirst for knowledge was always a pleasure to see. Fortunately, there are teachers in many schools who also understand the importance of Nature.

The need for stimulating science-oriented lectures and literature was also evident outside of university and school circles. Nature center personnel have always sought stimulating lecturers, field-trip leaders and reading material that will spark the interests of young nature-oriented participants, but they often have had difficulty in finding people and literature to accomplish this. Thus while on the Board of Directors at Sandy Creek Nature Center in Georgia, I worked with both teachers and young people and had taken part in many panel discussions to determine what it is that causes children to lose interest in science as they get older.

There is no doubt that young people still enjoy hearing about Nature, taking part in field trips and learning about the interactions of organisms in their natural environment, and it is young people who we should be approaching with information about our environmental problems. As Tony Shearer, in *The Praying Flute, Song of the Mother Earth*, put it, "you've got to go to the Children. The Children, the People of tomorrow, will become the guardians of the Earth."

The purpose of *The Magic of Nature* is to let our children know about Nature and the interesting lives of organisms that are found there. Its difference from many books is that it has been written in story-book fashion, allowing young students to enter an *Alice-in-Wonderland*-like fantasy world which, in actuality, is based on factual information.

In addition to the chapters, designed to provide information of an ecological, behavioral and anatomical nature, a glossary has been provided that identifies many of the terms and organisms mentioned in the book which students may want to understand a little better. On occasion, additional reading sources are recommended.

Preliminary copies of *The Magic of Nature* have been read in 5th grade classes, a chapter at a time. By the time it was completed, children learned not only to enjoy the story about Nature and the boy who experienced it, but they came away with new information about the organisms that they share Earth with.

Table of Contents

①

Nature Lures
Jason to the Country

Upon opening his eyes, Jason stared at an unfamiliar ceiling for several minutes. Still half asleep, he had to think really hard about where he was and what was in store for him during the upcoming day. Having spent the first night of his summer vacation at the country home of his Uncle Ted and Aunt Sarah, he was hoping he would have a chance to experience some quality time with his cousin, David.

Although Jason had spent time with his relatives the year before, it had been a while since they were all together, and he was a little apprehensive about being amongst people who weren't accustomed to the way he lived and functioned in a city environment.

He was like many of his friends. Quite a lot of his daily activity during the school year was devoted to homework, but much of his spare time was

1

spent amongst his friends at the controls of popular electronic games. And when he wasn't with a number of them, he was often at home doing similar types of things.

He and his friends were very active as young boys and girls, periodically fitting not only the routine features of daily life into their schedules but various other activities as well. For city kids, this was their daily life. Yet, he had a deep-seated desire to do something he wasn't accustomed to, something that had been on his mind for quite some time, such as spending time with and learning about the natural world. For some reason, he dreamed about consorting with animals in the wild.

Nature, his teacher had told him, is not on the minds of many people in cities these days because everyone was more involved in doing their city jobs. Even with the limited contact he had with nature in the city, though, he had developed more than a casual interest in it, and spending time in a country setting was a chance to be as close to nature as he could be.

The contrast between city living and country living was significant, he thought. Even after spending a single night at the farm, it was obvious that he would experience a variety of nature that had never even entered his thoughts. This excited him.

As he drifted into sleep the night before, he was serenaded by the faint calls of what sounded like thousands of frogs and toads at nearby ponds and the nocturnal sounds of owls and whip-o-wills in trees close to the house. As he awoke, the sounds of nature competed with the animal language that sprang from the nearby barn. It was already starting out as a day very different from those he was used to.

While not accustomed to being around animals, Jason had been interested in wildlife ever since he first spotted a small, round, brightly-colored beetle gobbling up tiny insects in the flower garden of his city home. What an appetite it had! Being the most unusual behavior he'd ever seen, he watched as it devoured insect after insect, finally spreading its wings and flying to another plant to gobble up some more.

At the library, he learned that the small insects on the plant he was observing were called aphids and that they sometimes hurt the plants they fed upon by sucking out liquids from the plant's tissues. The types of insects that were feeding on the aphids were called ladybird beetles. They helped the plant by eating aphids that were hurting it. Reading further, he learned that there were all kinds of similar relationships between these and other creatures that he knew very little or nothing about.

A ladybird beetle has spread its wings to fly. It has two pairs of wings. The front ones (the ones in this picture that have black dots on them) are covers for the second pair. When ready to fly, the second pair unfolds, and when their flight is finished, they are folded back again, and the first pair is moved back over them.

A lizard called an anole, showing it extending its dewlap, a device which it uses to show other anoles that the place it occupies (its territory) belongs to him.

Searching for further insect activity in the garden, he suddenly noticed a green lizard on the fence, pumping its body up and down as if it was doing push-ups and extending its pink spring-like dewlap from its neck. Standing motionless, he watched as the lizard subsequently tilted its head to one side, rushed to a moth fluttering on the ground, and devoured it in a split second. It licked its scaly lips with its pink tongue when it was finished. He subsequently spent countless hours in the garden, watching insects and other critters as they went about their daily activities.

On one of the days he was especially interested in watching nature, one of his best friends, John, was becoming bored with Jason's activities and said, "What are you watching those dumb insects for? Let's go play some games."

"Wait, John. Look at this!" He pointed to a black wasp that was carrying what appeared to be a paralyzed caterpillar to its nest. Oddly, the first pair of its six legs supported the caterpillar beneath its body while it walked on the other four.

A predatory wasp carrying its caterpillar prey to its nest. It has stung the caterpillar. When it puts the caterpillar in its nest, it lays an egg on it. The wasp larva will feed on the caterpillar and eventually emerge as a new adult wasp.

"I read about these in one of my books," he said enthusiastically, hoping John would become more interested in what he had found. "The wasp has stung the caterpillar. It is going to lay an egg on the caterpillar when it reaches its nest, and the young worm-like stage of the wasp is going to eat it." He and John watched until it crawled into a hole, wishing they could see inside.

It was after those first encounters with nature that reading about and observing the unusual lives of animals became one of his favorite past-times. Ants, bees, spiders, snakes, raccoons, the usual and unusual, all were fascinating to him, although he couldn't see them all in the city.

In spite of his new-found interest, though, he occasionally became distracted from his fascination with nature by events in the world around him. Since his friends remained more enchanted with the world of electronics, he retained an interest in it as well, and they often spent a considerable amount of their time playing video games and texting one another. He had to admit that electronics played a significant role of their lives. He, like his friends, also spent time watching his favorite television programs, corresponding with his friends through the internet, and listening to his favorite tunes on his ipod.

Nevertheless, he couldn't help returning to thoughts about the world of nature. There was something about nature's creatures that fascinated him, but living in the city isolated him from ones he could see in a more natural setting.

That's why he became so excited when his aunt called and invited him to their country farm. What made it even better, his cousin, David, would be home from college and was going to take him on his very first field trip.

The minute he heard, he began gathering up clothes and other belongings that he wanted to take. He had about a week to prepare for his visit, and his time was spent almost entirely with getting ready and reading about creatures he may find. His mother dropped him off at the farm on the evening of the day that school ended.

Detecting faint voices in the kitchen on the morning after their arrival, he jumped out of bed, quickly dressed, threw some water on his face, brushed his teeth, ran downstairs, and entered the kitchen, not quite awake but with a broad smile on his face. He greeted his aunt and uncle with a cheery, "Good Morning."

"Good morning, Jason!" they said, smiling back.

While his aunt busied herself with making breakfast, his uncle sat at the table, having a cup of hot coffee. Because his aunt and uncle always enjoyed doing most of their chores before the day got too hot, they usually ate breakfast very early in the morning. However, since both he and his cousin, David, were at the farm on this particular occasion, his uncle had returned to the house after having done some of his chores so they could all eat together.

"Did you sleep well?" his aunt asked. "I hope the bed was comfortable enough."

"Yes, it was great, Aunt Sarah. Thanks. I can't remember when I slept any better. I was so tired last night, I don't even remember going to bed."

They had stayed up late because it was the first time they had all been together for a while, and there was a lot to talk about. It was during the evening that David had told them some of the things he had learned at college, and this put Jason in a frame of mind that excited him more. He was certain to learn some new information about nature while they were together.

"Well, I hope you're rested. You have a long day ahead of you," his aunt said.

As his aunt continued talking, he drifted into thoughts of his own. He suspected that there were all sorts of creatures in the fields and woods surrounding the farm, and in anticipation of possibly visiting their farm, Jason had spent many hours in the library throughout the year, going through books about animals indigenous to these parts and reading about Native Americans who had once lived there. Acknowledging his sincere interest in nature, his parents had given him a field guide to reptiles and amphibians and another on insects and spiders so he could identify some of the creatures he found.

Living in the city and being limited in what he could observe in nature was what kept him thinking about visiting his aunt and uncle throughout the entire school year. He was sure that a day hadn't gone by that he didn't think about it.

②

Contemplating a Learning Experience

Looking directly at his aunt, Jason asked, "Aunt Sarah, what kinds of animals are out in the woods and fields here?" Most of his animal watching on his brief visit the year before had been limited to domestic animals around the house and barn.

"Well, let's see," she said. "I don't know them all, but there are deer, raccoons, possums, foxes, rabbits, and squirrels. I'll bet if you look outside right now you'll see a squirrel or two. We see them all the time. In fact, I feed them on occasion, and that keeps them coming around. We like to see them in our yard."

Jason ran to the window and peered outside, and, sure enough, two squirrels were searching for food on the back porch. He watched them scurry along, their fluffy tails swaying rhythmically with their movements. To him, they were beauty in motion.

Squirrels are mammals that belong to the rodent group, including tree squirrels, ground squirrels, chipmunks, marmots. Mammals are animals with a backbone, and they produce milk for feeding their young. They also have fur or hair, and three small bones in their ears.

"Wow!" he said, his eyes fixed on their every movement.

As he watched them running about, his aunt continued. "There are a number of different snakes in the woods, like corn and king snakes, and water snakes down by the lake. Some of their patterns and colors are absolutely beautiful." She hesitated for a moment, thinking.

"There also are blue racers, garter snakes, and a few others here and there. Once in a while, we see them in our yard. I'm sure there are many I haven't seen, but I'll bet David will show you a few. He's looking forward to going on this trip with you."

Jason smiled and then thought about his fear of snakes, a fear that he attributed to his lack of knowledge about them. Being unfamiliar with which ones were poisonous, he stayed away from most of them. Yet, he had a sincere desire to learn about their lives, as well, because he understood they were animals too. As he thought, he heard his aunt adding even more to the list of animals that frequented the area.

"There are a lot of different kinds of birds," she said. "The biggest ones are hawks, vultures and owls, and I shouldn't forget the herons, ibises, and egrets by the lake. They are so beautiful and graceful, especially during their breeding season. The purple gallinule is a spectacular species and one of my favorites. We've seen an eagle or two throughout the years, and we occasionally hear their calls, but they are rare."

Snakes are reptiles that lack legs. There are venomous and non-venomous types, and in the United States, the non-venomous types far outnumber the venomous ones. In places like Australia, however, there are numerous venomous ones.

Ibises are rather strange looking wading bird with a long down-curved bill, long neck, and long legs. They mostly feed in shallow waters on aquatic insects, mollusks, frogs, and food sifted from the water surface.

"Aren't there a lot of smaller birds in the woods too?" Jason asked.
"I don't know all the little birds, but there are warblers, mocking

birds, robins, blue birds, sparrows, and others that you can watch at the bird feeder. My favorite is the painted bunting, with its green, blue, yellow and red feathers. Have you seen one of those?"

"No, I haven't," said Jason, trying to imagine such a brightly-colored bird in his mind, "but I would like to. There sure are a lot of different kinds of birds here."

"The varieties of birds we see are most different in the spring and fall of the year," she said, "because that's when they migrate.

"If you go down by the lake," his aunt continued, "there's an area that's like a swamp, and you can see all kinds of frogs, toads, and salamanders there. You probably heard them last night before you fell asleep."

A frog (left), toad (middle) and salamander (right), all members of a group called amphibians because they live on land but must deposit their eggs in water. Some salamanders spend their entire life in water.

Jason acknowledged that he had heard them by shaking his head affirmatively.

" Also, there are many different kinds of fish in the lake."

Jason asked, "Do you think I'll see some of those animals while I'm here, Aunt Sarah?"

"I wouldn't be surprised. The weather is nice and warm. If you don't see anything else, you'll see lots of insects and spiders. You may want to put on some insect spray before you leave."

When David entered the room, Jason got a giant smile on his face. As he greeted Jason and his parents, everyone sat at the table and had breakfast. After discussing the weather and commenting about how beautiful the day was going to be, his aunt asked, "Are you ready to take Jason on his field trip, David?"

David jumped from his chair and answered as he left the room, "Hold on, I'll be ready in just a few minutes, Mom. I have to get a few things to take along with us." When he returned a few minutes later, carrying several items in his hands, he looked at Jason and asked, "What kind of a field trip do you want to go on, Jason?"

David's question confused Jason, making him wonder how many kinds of field trips there were.

Noticing his confused expression, David said, "The direction we go in and the things I show you depend on what you'd like to see."

An insect is an animal without a backbone. They develop through different stages (such as a caterpillar or other type of immature stage), and they have six legs, a head, thorax, and abdomen in the adult stage.

His aunt and uncle picked up the breakfast dishes, leaving the two boys to plan their day together.

Jason looked inquisitively at his cousin and said "Well, I'd just like to see some animals, David. I don't get to see wild animals where I live, so I don't really know that much about them. Mostly what I've seen are a few insects and lizards that live in the garden, and once in a while I see rats around dumpsters."

"Then, let me ask you another question," said David, this time probing to see what Jason understood about nature. "Do you know how all the animals fit into nature? There's a delicate relationship between all of them, you know."

"I've read about the lives of animals in nature and the lNative Americans who lived amongst them, but I don't understand what you mean," Jason said. "How are they all related? Is it like you and me, cousins or something?"

"No, not really," David responded, a slight smile on his face. "Let's see, how will we start?" He thought for a moment and said, "I'll tell you what we'll do," a sound of enthusiasm in his voice.

He pulled out a pen and began drawing a crude map of the area on a piece of paper. "We'll take a trip from here," pointing to their house on his map, "and go through the fields to a wooded area. Then we'll head through the swamp and toward the lake. That way, we'll experience different habitats, and I'll try to explain about the plants and animals as we see them."

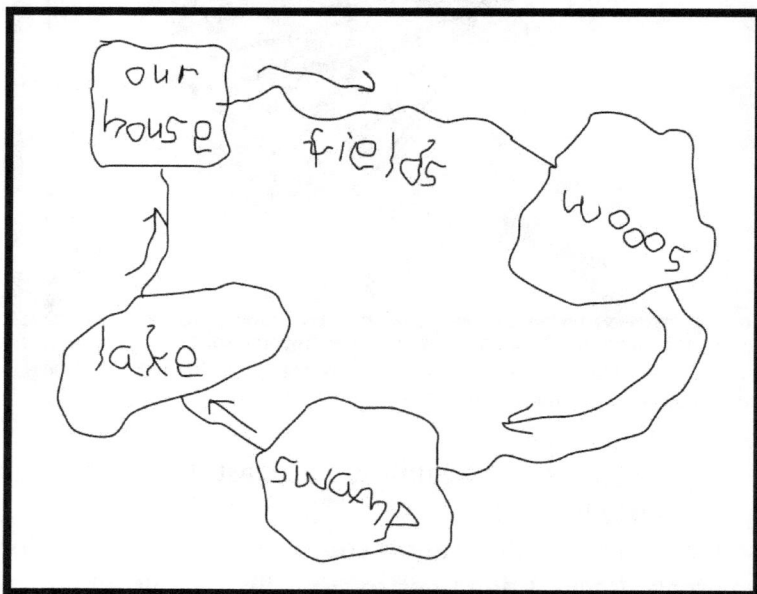

Before leaving, David conversed with Jason at length about the different areas they would venture into and the animals they might find, often making reference to the map he'd drawn. With excitement building in him like the pressure in a steam engine, Jason listened attentively and attempted to tie together the information David was providing with what he had read. At this point, some of what David said was somewhat confusing.

"Don't worry, Jason. When we get into the field, things will become clearer to you, and I'll repeat the information I feel you should know."

When he felt he had properly prepared Jason for their forthcoming excursion and given the sun enough time to warm the various habitats they would visit, David asked, "Are you ready to visit nature, Jason?"

"I sure am!" he answered, his face lighting up with anticipation.

Handing Jason a back pack and a potato rake and holding onto another pair for himself, David said "You may need these two items."

Looking curiously at them, Jason asked, "What are they for?"

"Well, the back pack contains some lunch for us, water, a few tools, and several plastic bags, in case we want to collect anything, and I like to carry a potato rake with me to roll logs and rocks. They come in handy. It beats putting your hands in places where something may bite or sting you. We'll also take an insect net to catch some of the things we see."

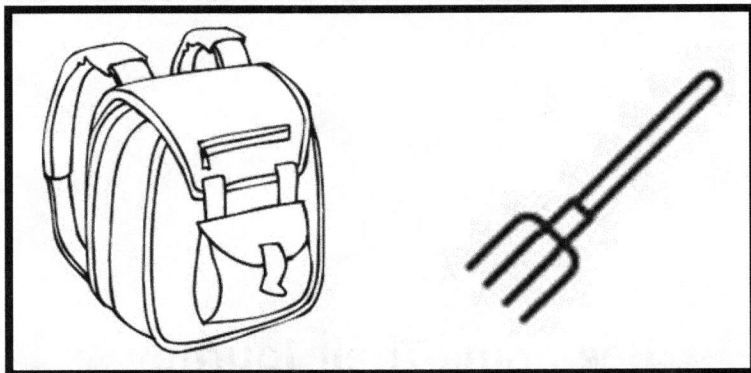

Back packs can be used to keep jars, field guides, and many other things. Potato rakes are handy for lifting stones and rolling small logs to see what is beneath them.

As Jason examined the net and rake and fitted the back pack over his shoulders, David saw excitement in his expression, reminding him of himself when he was that age. Smiling, he said, "Okay Jason, let's get started." They turned and headed out the door.

"Be careful, and have fun," his aunt called as they left.

③

Beginning Their Journey

I t couldn't have been a better day for a field trip, being warm, with a very slight breeze. The smell of fresh air was something he was not accustomed to at home. The sun shone brightly in a magnificent blue sky, and the sparse clouds were the light, fluffy cumulus types that lazily float through the sky on a beautiful summer day.

The dew that had settled on the vegetation and the water that the plants had produced during the night were now evaporating, and the sun was casting a warm glow over the field they were about to enter. After David briefly explained to Jason how all the plants breathe in a chemical called carbon dioxide through their leaves, make their own food with help from the sunlight and produce oxygen that all animals breathe, photosynthesis he called it, they entered the field and immediately were confronted with a large variety of insects.

Cumulus clouds, very common during the summer. They are low clouds that are made up of steam and build up from the evaporation of water on the Earth. When they get large and the water particles in them become dense enough, much of the steam in clouds can turn back into liquid water, and it rains.

Two good tools to take on a field trip to help with looking closely at the things you see.

Jason was immediately amazed by the variety of sounds he heard around them. As they stepped into the field, numerous grasshoppers suddenly jumped up from the plants they had been resting and feeding upon and flew in various directions, making sudden thrashing sounds as they left their plants and then clattering sounds as they flew away. When Jason and

David moved to a new location in the field, the sounds repeated themselves.

Not being able to see above the tall grasses, Jason imagined himself in a mysterious jungle, surrounded by all types of wild plants and animals. He couldn't look around without seeing something interesting.

The variety of insects they saw was far beyond his wildest expectations. In fact, he couldn't remember ever having seen so many different creatures in one place, and because of the net and a magnifying glass that David had brought, Jason, for the first time in his life, was able to examine the details of their incredible anatomy.

Variations in body shapes and size, as well as the presence of spines, hairs, and other rather strange but fascinating extensions from their hard integuments were unceasingly different. Colors ran the gamut from subdued tans, browns and blacks to bright reds, yellows, greens, blues, and purples, the surface of their integuments sometimes even appearing metallic. As soon as David caught an insect and discussed it at length with Jason, he released it back into the field, caught another and repeated the process.

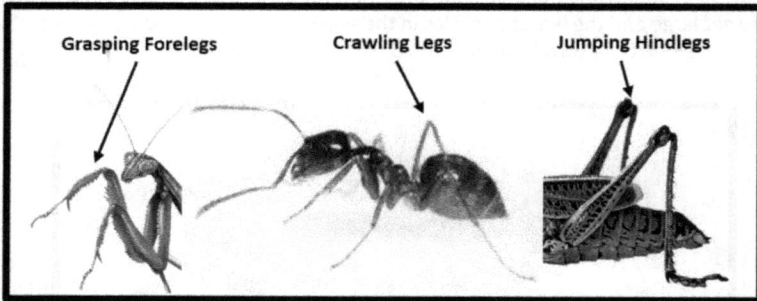

Different types of insect legs. Left, the grasping forelegs (front legs) of mantids are used to catch and eat other insects and their relatives. Center, crawling legs like those found in many insects. Right, jumping hindlegs, as seen in grasshoppers and crickets.

Coupled with anatomical diversity (different body styles), widely divergent behavioral differences helped Jason understand that no two types of animals (species) in nature were exactly the same. Such differences and food preferences kept each species separate in their habitat. Winged varieties could easily move from plant to plant while non-winged forms had to walk, crawl, or jump from one place to another.

Some lived solitary lives while others were social, their young, like human infants, requiring special care. Some fed on plant material, while others fed upon one another, their differences often being expressed in a variety of distinct sounds.

Noticing Jason's focus on the various creatures that they examined, David took a minute to watch him, finally asking, "Jason, are you enjoying our field trip so far?"

"I sure am!" Jason replied, the sound of excitement very evident in his voice. "I didn't know there were so many different kinds of animals out here and that their lives were so interesting! I really would like to come out here every day!"

Tiger beetle adult. Some have patterns that make them blend into their environment (they are cryptic) while others have various patterns that show up as metallic greens. They are predaceous (they catch and eat other insects).

After David explained that some of the fastest flying insects were certain flies, beetles, moths and butterflies, and that one of the fastest insects was a small insect called a tiger beetle, Jason wondered about the reasons for variations in the speeds at which different animals traveled. *It may have to do with quickly catching their prey*, he thought, *but it may also have something to do with escaping from other things that may eat them*. He also contemplated the reasons behind size variation and the use of their sounds.

The ground surrounding the plants was busy with crawling critters of various sorts, like long legged beetles, ants, centipedes, millipedes, daddy-long-legs and spiders, most of which Jason had not seen or heard of before.

Forming an unusual spectacle as they scurried around, it was as though he was high up in the sky or on a mountaintop, viewing the population of people scurrying about far below in a distant valley.

By the time they left the field, they had seen many types of insects, a couple of snakes had slithered past them and a fox had run by. Through it all, David presented Jason with facts about each and every one of them, pointing to pictures in Jason's field guides whenever possible.

Overhead, a number of birds of various sizes flew by. Turkey buzzards silently circled high in the sky, taking advantage of the summer air currents to lift them to unbelievable heights without having to even flap their wings. Crows, grackles, and smaller blackbirds flew over in flocks of varying sizes, making loud calls as if to say, "There are fields down below with all kinds of food for us. Let's go down and get some."

Many smaller birds flew close to the field, darting in and out of the plants. Occasionally, one or more of them landed to feed on seeds and insects that were scurrying about. While some flew in large flocks, others flew in smaller groups or alone, each type with a different song to sing. With their melodious squawking, the buzzing of insects, and the sporadic swishing sounds of grass and other plants moving in the wind, it was sometimes quite noisy, but a pleasant and exciting kind of noisy. David referred to it as "Nature's Orchestra." He could close his eyes, and based on the sounds he heard, he could imagine what activity was going on around him.

Left, a black buzzard (vulture), one of the buzzards that fly in circles, looking for dead animals to feed upon. Right, a cara cara, another bird that feeds upon dead animals.

As he listened, David commented, "Those sounds you hear amongst the low vegetation are mostly sounds of grasshoppers and other insects flying by. Do you hear them in the city?"

"Oh, no," Jason answered. "I never get to hear all of this in the city. What I hear mostly are horns and sirens."

A raccoon, a medium-sized mammal native to North America. Its grayish coat of hair mostly consists of dense underfur which insulates it against cold weather. They are omnivores (they will eat just about anything) and they function mostly at night (they are nocturnal).

As they moved to the far end of the field, the scenery began to change to a less-grassy habitat with larger shrubs and bushes. Spending a little time by the edge of the woodland, they looked under logs and conversed about the differences in the types of vegetation that existed between this area and the one they had just visited. Jason was quick to observe that many of the insects and other animals here were also different from those they had seen in the open field.

It was here that they saw a raccoon run into its rocky den and several different snakes slowly slithering by. While many of the noises of the field were lacking here, there were insects and birds moving about in what appeared to be a more silent fashion.

④

Changing Habitats

U pon entering the woodland area, Jason immediately recognized a more silent environment and felt the eerie sensation of darkness caused by the large tree tops and branches overhead (the canopy). Occasionally, filtered sunlight squeezed through rare holes in the canopy to brighten patches on the forest floor. The sounds they heard bouncing off the trees were distinctly different from ones they had already experienced.

Jason turned to David and asked, "Why do I feel things are not the same here as in the places we've been? There's something different, but I don't exactly know what it is."

"That's because it's a very different kind of habitat," David answered, "and the animals and plants are very different too. It's good that you noticed,

Jason. Most people don't realize there are differences."

Warmth from the sun brings out insects that cannot function very well when it is cool. Unlike people, insects are generally unable to produce their own body heat.

Instead of the loud thrashing, buzzing and clattering sounds of insects and the telltale signs of birds in the field, he heard mostly the swishing of the wind through the trees and occasional haunting squeaks of trees rubbing upon one another. When he closed his eyes, he felt an inner peace, the only sounds of animal life being the high pitched squeal of a distant hawk as it circled overhead, the cawing of distant crows, and the occasional chattering of a woodpecker as it flew from tree to tree. The woodpecker's short, wavering flights culminated with the noise of pounding made by its beak as it searched for sap and insects within the trees' tissues.

For the first time on their trip, deer flies circled their heads, their wings making an annoying buzzing sound that was distinct from the sounds of bees and other flying insects. Occasionally, flies landed on their skin, and David and Jason experienced the burning sensations of their bites.

Suddenly, Jason remembered what his aunt had said about using an insect repellent. "Boy! I wish we remembered to bring the bug spray."

"Yeah," agreed David. "That would have made it a lot more pleasant out here. We're kind-of-like an insect feeding station."

Jason laughed.

Passing through a swamp adjacent to a freshwater lake, mosquitoes became an issue, and the thought of not having an insect spray resurfaced in Jason's mind. Their slight but persistent humming noises, distinctly different from the buzzing of other flies in the woodland area, were annoying enough without the stinging pain that went along with it. While he understood that mosquitoes were animals too, he wasn't sure he would ever learn to appreciate the experience he was having with them as they attempted to take his blood.

Flailing his arms and slapping his skin, Jason said, "Boy, these mosquitoes are really annoying! Why do they have to bother us so much, David?"

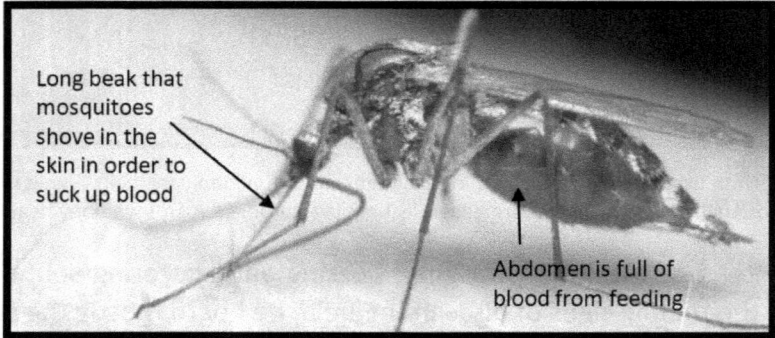

Long beak that mosquitoes shove in the skin in order to suck up blood

Abdomen is full of blood from feeding

Mosquito adult, feeding on the blood of a human. Only female mosquitoes suck blood. Males sometimes feed on nectar from flowers.

"Mosquitoes have to suck blood," David answered. "That's the only way they can eat. If females don't get a blood meal, they can't lay eggs." This was apparently enough of a question from Jason to get David talking about these and other types of animals that have to feed on other animals, parasites as David called them.

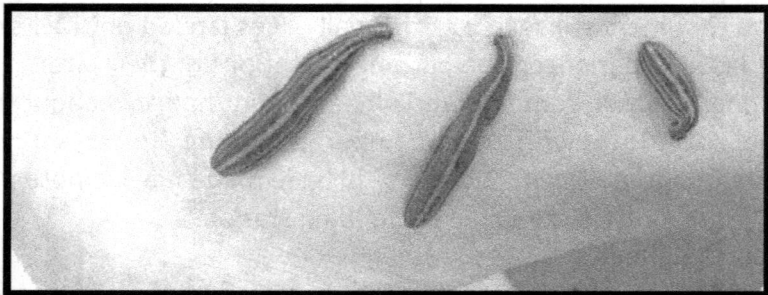

Leeches are parasites that suck blood out of their host. When they feed, they produce a numbing chemical that keeps the pain of feeding to a minimum, and they also produce anticoagulents to keep the blood flowing during feeding.

When they walked through some of the tannin-rich swamp water,

pleasant at first because of the cool, soothing feeling on their feet, an occasional leech latched onto their ankles and began to suck their blood. What
was amazing to Jason about these strange, worm-like animals was that he
didn't feel their bite, and he wasn't even aware of their presence until the
water became shallow enough for him to see them clinging to his ankles.

Although he enjoyed it when David went into even more detail about
the lives of these swamp inhabitants, as well as insects, ticks, mites, and
other creatures that feed upon other animals, he was glad when they got
out into the open and upon dry land again. It was here that they finally got
to enjoy the absence of biting flies. With a little patience, they were able to
remove the leeches and stop the flow of blood that oozed out of the feeding
sites.

When they reached the lake, Jason could immediately tell that the
plants and animals were again quite different. There were plants that appeared to actually prefer growing in the water. Large birds, such as herons,
egrets, and ibises, slowly walked and fed along the water's edge, expressing
their various feeding and stalking behaviors. Numerous dragonflies of varying sizes flew back and forth overhead.

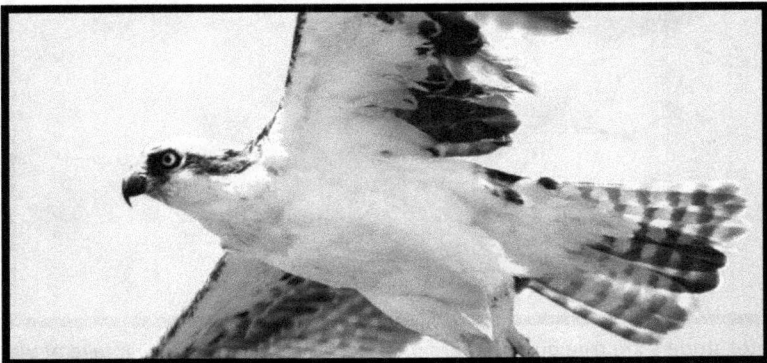

An osprey, a bird that feeds on fish, is often seen flying around ponds and lakes
where it can swoop down and grab fish in its sharp, pointed talons (long and
strong toenails).

"Look up, Jason!" David yelled. "See that bird hovering overhead?
That's an osprey. It's looking for a fish."

Just as Jason looked to where David was pointing, the bird swooped down to the water and brought up a fish in its talons. "Wow, that's so amazing!" shouted Jason. Landing on a near-by post, the bird proceeded to eat the fish while Jason and David watched.

Moving closer to the water to determine what was causing some ripples in the surface, Jason saw fish swimming by and different types of insects skimming across the top of the water's surface, some of the insects performing a dance-like routine.

Noticing that Jason had a fascination with these insects, David said, "Those are water striders, Jason. They have tiny hydrophobic (water-repelling) hairs on their feet that allow them to walk on water, and the tiny waves that they make help them communicate with one another.

"Wow," Jason said, moving closer to watch.

Jason was beginning to realize even more than he suspected that the animal and plant world was very complex. Everything seemed to be doing something different in nature, and they all seemed to interact in one way or another.

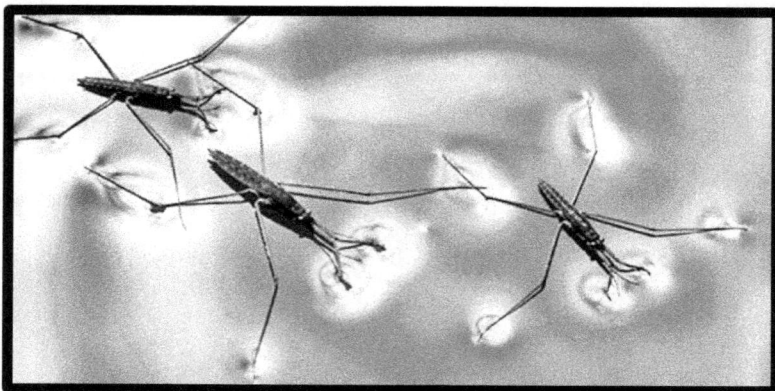

Water striders are true bugs that are predators that can taking advantage of water's surface tension and hydrophobic (water repellent) hairs that allow them to standing on water. When they move, the moving water surface plays a role in their spacing and their behavioral displays.

⑤

Concluding Their Journey

I t was by the lake that they sat and had their lunch. When he looked into the bag, Jason smiled, seeing a peanut-butter sandwich on home-made bread and a container of chocolate pudding. As they sat and ate, they talked about the things they had seen, and David found this to be a good time to repeat some of the information about nature that he felt was espe-cially important.

When they finished, they put the sandwich bags and cups back into their back packs so they could dispose of them when they returned to the house. This gave David a chance to talk about how important it is to not pol-lute the environment, to pick up trash and other things that would interfere with keeping nature clean.

David said, "The only things we should leave in nature are our foot prints." Jason smiled and checked around to make sure they had left the environment with no trace of their presence.

The remainder of the afternoon was spent heading back toward the house. During this part of the adventure, they saw even more different animals and plants, and David caught a snake and explained about its life amongst all the other animals.

"Look at this, Jason," David said. "The pupils in the eye of this snake are round, just as they are in most non-poisonous snakes. The pupil of most poisonous snakes in the United States have an elliptical shape." Pointing to the tongue flicking in and out of the snake's mouth, he said, "The snake's forked tongue helps it sense its environment."

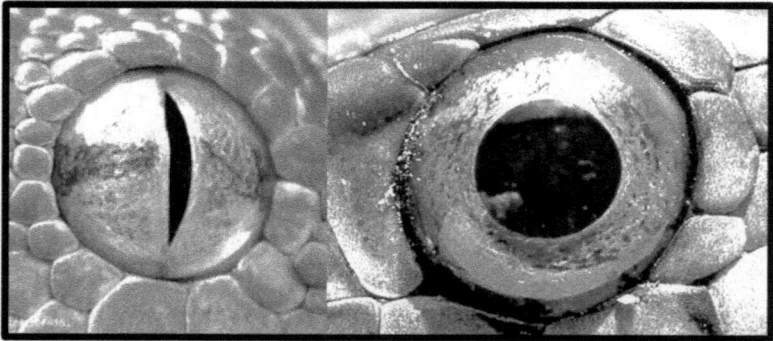

Most venomous snakes in the United States have elliptical pupils (as seen on the left), with the exception of the coral snake, while non-venomous snake eyes have round pupils. When considering the snakes of the world, however, this rule may not apply.

Finding a bird's nest in a shrub and some snake eggs under a log, David let Jason feel how soft and rubbery the snake eggs were, and he talked about the difference between them and bird eggs. Jason just shook his head and wondered if there was ever an end to the variety of things they would find.

Completing their trip through all the different areas and talking about the plants and animals that were there, Jason's head was spinning with new facts. He had never received so much information in such a short time in his life, not realizing that David had not finished with the learning session.

When they arrived back at the house, David sat down with Jason over a cold glass of iced tea and tied together many of the thoughts and concepts he had mentioned to him on their trip. In addition to explaining a little more about the plants and the lives of the animals they had seen, David related the importance of each one and how they all fit into the environment.

"I hope you had a nice time on our trip today, Jason. It was a good day to observe nature. And I enjoyed being with you."

"I had a really good time," Jason replied. "I learned more about nature today than I ever have before. Thanks, David."

"We've seen many different things today, Jason, and I believe you realize that each place we went had different kinds of plants and animals. This is not accidental. You see, all these different plants and animals belong to particular habitats, and they are all important to one another."

Jason looked a little puzzled and said, "Would you explain about habitats again, David?"

"A habitat is a certain place where animals and plants live, like the grass field we went through. That's a grassland habitat, and it has certain plants and animals that live in it. When we left the grassland habitat, we entered a habitat called a woodland edge, and it has its own types of plants and animals. Of course, there's some overlap between the two.

"Then we went into a woodland habitat and a swamp habitat, each of which has certain types of plants and animals. Finally, we went by a freshwater habitat, and you could see again that the plants and animals there were quite different. Sometimes, these plants and animals can live in more than one type of habitat, but it's the combination of different plants and animals, as well as the air, water, temperature, and many other things that make up a particular habitat.

"What people sometimes don't understand is that these habitats are very delicate, and the animals and plants that live in them are dependent upon each other and their relationship with their habitat to stay alive and reproduce. When we destroy a habitat, say to build something or to clear it away to plant crops, we not only eliminate the habitat, we also eliminate all the plants and animals that are associated with them.

"When we eliminate the plants and animals from one habitat, we may cause changes in other habitats as well."

Frowning, Jason asked, "How does that happen?"

"Well, let's see. Maybe I can give you an example. Suppose we decide to fill in this lowland area and build houses all over it. To do that, we'd eliminate the grassland and woodland habitats. The plants that live in each of those habitats would no longer have a home, and all the insects and other animals that live there wouldn't have a home either because they feed on the plants and other creatures that are familiar to that habitat."

Still a little puzzled, Jason asked, "But why don't the insects and other animals just move to another habitat?"

"That's a really good question, Jason. It's true that they sometimes can move to another habitat, but most of the time they don't. They live in a particular habitat because the food they eat and other things they require are there, and they have developed a sort-of-a balance with the community that has taken many years to establish.

"Changes in habitats affect other areas as well. For instance, the water that flows across the ground and through streams in these habitats would change, and this would change the lake that the water flows into. When the lake changes, the plants and animals in it change as well."

Their discussion went on for another half-an-hour, David realizing that Jason had gotten to a point of being saturated with the information he had given him. Jason's eyelids now drooping, he thanked David again for a wonderful day and for all the information he had given him, but David noticed a worried look on Jason's face.

"What's the matter, Jason?"

"Well, I'm not sure I can remember all the things you've told me. My head is spinning with all this new knowledge, and it's making me real tired."

David laughed, knowing exactly what Jason was talking about. Understanding the concept of an environment with all its living and non-living components was a difficult thing to do, especially for a young boy who had never had the opportunity to experience it all before.

Patting him on his shoulder, David said, "Just sleep on it, Jason, and maybe some of the things will come back to you. It's not important to remember everything right now. We can always talk about it some more, and there will be other field trips to go on."

David suddenly wondered if he had gone overboard with the information he gave Jason. Maybe it would have been better to spread it out over two or three days, maybe even a week. As he continued to think about it, he confessed to himself that it really had been a special day, a day that was perfect for observing nature. It was almost as though it was a day made just for Jason.

After showering and eating supper, Jason yawned a few times, helped clear the table, said good night, and went upstairs to his room. Falling upon the bed, and launching into thoughts about his day's adventure, he reminisced about the facts that David had given him and the many sounds he had heard. Somehow, he felt his life had changed in that single day. With these facts now spinning around in his head like nothing he had ever experienced, he quickly fell into a deep sleep.

⑥

The Grasshopper

A s Jason faded off into a deep sleep, he began to have a most bizarre dream about his adventures that day. Suddenly, he was back in the field that he and David had been in after leaving the house that morning, and he was again surrounded by all the plants and animals they had seen.

The grass was again making that swishing sound when the wind blew, and he heard the thrashing and clattering noises of grasshoppers taking off and scattering to other spots in the field. There was also the occasional buzzing of wings that so impressed him on the earlier trip.

Some outstanding differences between his previous trip with David and this one were not easy to understand, the most obvious of which was that insects and other animals were often as big as he was.

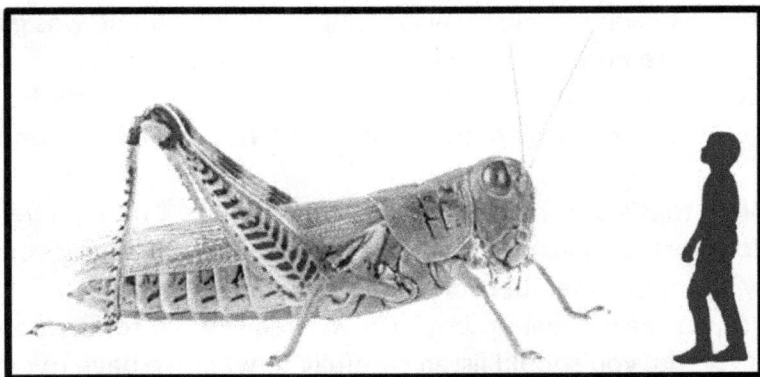

Jason couldn't believe how big all the animals were. It was certainly a circumstance he had never experienced before. And those weren't the only similarities between him and the insect that stood before him.

In addition, he was all alone in terms of human companions. He didn't know how he'd gotten out in the field, how the animals had grown to such a large size or where David had gone, but here he was, standing in the very high grass amongst all the living things he loved.

Looking around, he noticed other differences as well. Sounds were even more pronounced than they had been earlier, making him feel even closer to nature.

As he came upon a grasshopper of tremendous size, he stared at it and attempted to recall what David had told him about them and the habitats in which grasshoppers live. Upon carefully approaching the insect, he was surprised that it didn't fly away like the others had done. In fact, it didn't seem to be afraid of him at all. As it appeared to be looking directly at him with its large, complicated eyes, he began to wonder just what was on its mind, if anything.

Suddenly, the grasshopper asked, "What are you doing out here, boy? Aren't you supposed to be home, doing things that other humans do?"

Startled and a little afraid, Jason quickly concluded that what was happening was impossible. *Grasshoppers can't talk.* He looked at the grasshopper for a minute and with a slight uncertainty in his voice, he asked, "Wha…, What did you say, grasshopper?"

"I said, what are you doing here? I think I said it plainly enough."

Jason couldn't believe it! He was actually talking to a grasshopper, and it was responding with astounding clarity! It's the strangest feeling he had ever had! He was certain he was losing his mind, and he was glad none of his friends were here to witness such a bizarre conversation.

Nevertheless, not wanting to be rude and ignore the grasshopper, he said, "I'm out here to learn about the animals." He, of course, didn't expect a reply.

"Well, that's different," said the grasshopper. "That's a very noble thing to do. Most humans don't seem to care much about us, even though we're very important members of this community.

"Do you really mean it, boy? Do you really want to learn about us? Because if you do, you should listen carefully to what we have to say."

"Why yes, I really do want to learn about you and all the other animals. That's why I'm here. What do I have to do to convince you, grasshopper?" In the back of his mind, he still wasn't sure all this was happening.

"To learn about us," the grasshopper said, "you have to pay very close attention to each of us, because we all have an important story to tell. You see, we all have different roles in how nature works, and it's necessary that we all work together to get what we refer to as a balance.

"What do you mean, a balance?" Jason asked.

The grasshopper said, "It's the way that everything lives out here in nature so that we can all function together for the good of everyone.

"It's kind of interesting that humans of today talk about the balance, because they are very important in maintaining it too, but they do things to upset the balance every day. Maybe they're not as sincere as they think they are in how they feel about the environment. Maybe they should come out here and live with us for a while and talk to us like you're doing. You're going to find that if you talk to everyone out here in nature, you will begin to understand how this balance works and how important it is."

Now becoming more comfortable with the conversation, Jason said, "My cousin, David, has explained some of this to me, but I would appreciate hearing it from you. Maybe you could tell me what you're doing here in a grassy field?"

"Well," the grasshopper said, "I'd be happy to do that. I live here. I've always lived here, even when I was a little grasshopper without wings. My ancestors lived here too.

"Most grasshoppers like me live out in a field where we can hop and fly around and eat some of these plants. I don't usually stay around a forest or a lake, although I may go to the edge of a forest or the lake once in a while. The field is my primary habitat."

"I know what a habitat is," said Jason. My cousin told me about it. But if this is your habitat, what are you doing living with other types of animals? Is it their habitat too?"

"Why yes, it is. We share our habitat, but we each do different things in it."

"What do you mean, you do different things?" Jason asked.

"I may occupy a different spot in the habitat, eat things that are different from the food of the other animals here, my behavior may be different, or I may look or function in a different way."

"I have noticed that there were many different kinds of animals out here," said Jason. "You look a lot different from many of the others, but there are some that are very similar to you or have only a slightly different appearance. You don't look exactly like that grasshopper over there," he said, pointing to another type on a bush nearby.

"That's because that grasshopper is a different kind than I am. I'm called a short-horned grasshopper by you humans because my antennae are short when compared to the ones on that grasshopper, and I do things a little differently from that one."

"What do you mean?" Jason asked.

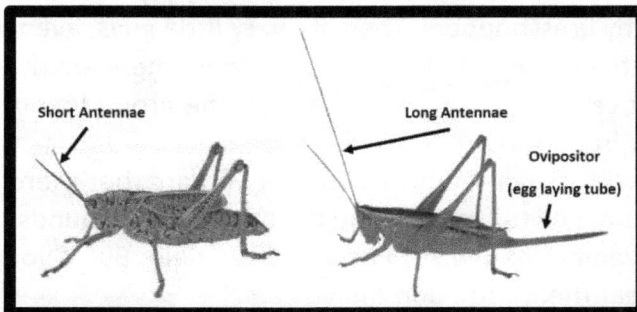

Left, a short horned grasshopper, showing its relatively short antennae, as compared to the much longer antennae on the long horned grasshopper to the right. In addition, long horned grasshoppers have a long ovipositor (egg laying tube).

"Well, that grasshopper is called a long-horned grasshopper because its antennae are very long. That long tube sticking out the tip of its abdomen is what it uses to lay its eggs. My species doesn't have one of those. We have other differences, too. My body is a lot more robust than its body. It sometimes flies up in trees or tall bushes or shrubs, and I usually don't go up there at all. I'd rather stay closer to the field.

"That grasshopper makes many of the evening sounds that you hear by rubbing its wings together, just like crickets do. Some humans call them katydids."

Jason said, "I've heard some of those sounds in the trees. What about you, though? Do you make sounds, too?"

"Oh, yes," the grasshopper said. "I make my sounds by rubbing my back legs against the side of my wings which produces more of a rasping sound, and when I fly, my wings beat together to produce a clattering sound. I'm sure you've heard all these sounds when you've walked through the fields."

"I certainly have," said Jason. "Those were some of the first sounds I noticed."

"I hop more than it does, and I often eat different foods than it does. While some of these differences appear to be minor, they often are important enough for us so that we don't have to compete for food or space out here in the field. So as you can see, we're quite different from one another in how we fit into nature.

"There also are other types of grasshoppers out here that you humans call pygmy grasshoppers. They are very little guys, even when they're grown up, but they look something like me. Then, there are the crickets who are close relatives, but they stay mostly on the ground, and their food is quite different from ours."

Jason said, "I can see how different you are, but there's one thing I can't understand. You tell me you and the others make sounds, and I do hear them in the evenings and when I'm out in the field. But if you make them, how do you hear them? You don't have ears."

Laughing, the grasshopper said, "Oh yes, we do have ears, but they look different from yours. You will not see them unless you look very closely. My ears are on the side of my abdomen." He turned sideways to show Jason his membrane-like ears.

"Long horned grasshopper's ears are on their front legs. You see, that's another difference between us."

Snickering a little, Jason said, "That's certainly a weird place to have ears, and they don't even look like ears."

Seeming a little disturbed by what Jason said, the grasshopper commented, "Well, I wouldn't laugh if I were you. I think your ears are the ones that look a little strange. You may be surprised to know that in spite of the fact that our ears are in a different place from yours and they look different, they work pretty much the same. Our ears are thin membranes that vibrate when sound waves hit them, very much like the membrane in your ear that you call an eardrum.

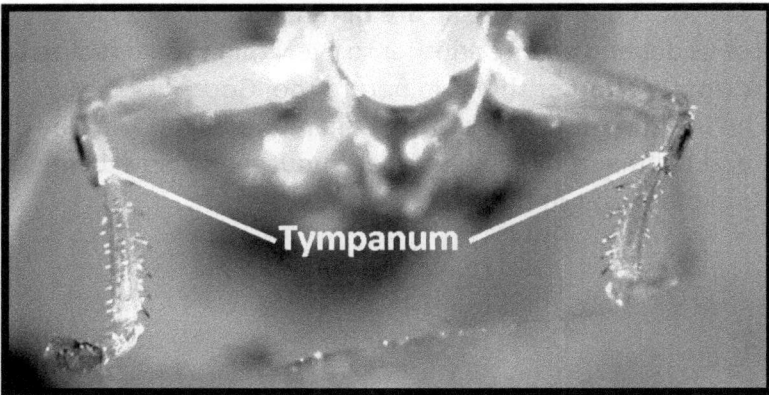

Longhorn grasshopper forelegs, showing the position of their tympanum (ear) on each tibia. The sounds they make are produced by rubbing their wings together.

"Most insects, like most other animals, have some types of hearing devices. Some moths' ears, for instance, are similar to ours, also being on the side of their body. Also, many hairs on insects are sensitive to vibrations produced by sounds. Sometimes our hearing is designed mostly for the sounds that we produce, but we most definitely can hear."

"What else do you do?" Jason asked.

"We have to be very careful out here. Sometimes, life isn't very pleasant. Birds sometimes eat us, and there are some other types of insects, like mantids, that eat us too. In some parts of the world, people even eat us. That's why we scatter when someone approaches. You never know who can cause you harm.

"Once in a while, we mate and lay eggs. I lay my eggs in a hole in the ground, but the long horned grasshopper usually lays its eggs in or on plants. Crickets often lay their eggs on the ground. When our young hatch, they don't have wings like we grown-ups have. They gradually get their wings after shedding their skin several times."

Noticing other insects flying around and not wanting to wear out his welcome, Jason said, "Well, thank you, grasshopper, for telling me all about yourself. I've learned a whole lot from you, and I've taken up enough of your time. I guess I just never took time to stop and look at you closely. I'll try to do this more in the future."

"I hope you will. You do have to look very closely sometimes, and when you do, you'll find that we all are different in one way or another and that many of us depend on one another to live. I think you'll realize this more as you look closely at other things in nature too. Good luck."

As he bid good-bye to Jason, he began to feed on a nearby plant, the crunching sounds made by his hardened mouthparts now being added to the other audible noises in the field.

⑦

The Honey Bee

With what he learned from the grasshopper, Jason walked further into the field, now even more enthusiastic and looking more closely at vegetation and other living things in his immediate vicinity. Because of all the activity around him, it was becoming confusing to focus on one particular subject, but he was determined not to miss anything that came to his attention.

As he examined the plants around him, he realized that the field was even more alive with a vast array of different kinds of insects than it had been on his trip with David. Not only were there numerous insects feeding on the leaves and stems of the plants, but some were feeding on the flowers as well, and others were flying in to get the sweet juice within the flowers that David had called nectar.

He watched them closely and noticed that when nectar-loving insects landed on a flower, they seemed to know exactly where to go to get the nectar. However, the way that they collected it varied with the type of insects visiting the flowers.

Insects that had long tube-like mouth parts especially adapted for getting nectar deep within the flower sucked the nectar up as we would suck up the liquid from a soft drink with a straw. He noticed that this was the method used by most of the bees and butterflies that visited the flowers.

Two types of insects that feed on nectar by sucking it from the flower through straw like mouthparts. The honey bee to the left readily takes nectar from most flowers but sometimes have difficulty in getting it from flowers that are long and slender. The proboscis of butterflies, however, is long enough to obtain nectar from most flower types.

A special kind of bee that David had called a carpenter bee demonstrated a most interesting manner of getting nectar. Since it had sharp mouthparts that it could use to cut with but lacked the long mouthparts to suck up liquids, it went to the base of a flower, cut a hole in a soft petal and lapped up the sweet nectar from the outside.

Nectar wasn't the only thing insects were interested in though. Some insects in the field were busy chewing the plant's leaves. Since they were as large as he was, he could distinctly hear their chewing, a sound that reminded him of when he bites into and chews a piece of celery. With the loud chewing, sucking, and buzzing all around, it was as noisy as being by a busy highway with the various sounds of cars and trucks all going this way and that.

Also, there were all kinds of strange behaviors being displayed by the insects. For example, when honey bees came in to get nectar, they hunkered down with their bodies and scooted around on the flower's surface to pick up pollen with the hairs that were so abundant on the surface of their body. Jason could easily see the tiny yellow pollen particles scattered around the bees' body. Periodically, they stopped picking up pollen and concentrated on scraping it off their yellow-speckled body with their legs, and it ended up in a depression on their third pair of legs that David called a pollen basket.

Rear view of a honey bee, showing pollen which has been collected from flowers while. It carries the pollen back to its nest in devices on its legs called pollen baskets, and they store it in the wax cells that they construct. In the process of removing nectar and pollen from the flower, they pollinate them.

The bees used their baskets to carry pollen back to their hives so their colony could feed on it. "It's their protein food," David had said. What was really important, though, was that when they scooted around at different flowers to pick up pollen, they left some pollen from previous flowers that they had visited.

By repeating the visits and the scooting behavior, they carried pollen from plant to plant, pollinating each flower that they visited in the process. This was how the plants made seeds that were surrounded by fruit and could eventually grow into new plants. He thought about how nicely nature had worked such a complex system out, and he understood that it was a wonderful and important way that plants and animals interacted.

Jason was so close to one particular enlarged bee that he could feel the wind from the rapid movements of its beating wings every time it became airborne. Also, the sound of its wings was sometimes so loud it reminded him of the sounds that came from an airplane propeller.

When the bee suddenly landed immediately in front of him, it folded its wings back over its body, dipped its long mouthparts into the flower base to get some nectar, moved back to the flower head, scooted around to get some pollen, and then appeared to look directly at him.

Rather than ignore the honey bee, Jason said, "Hello. Who are you?" Of course, he wasn't certain the bee would answer him as the grasshopper had done.

The bee stopped what it was doing, gave a surprised look in Jason's direction and said, "I'm a honey bee, if you must know."

Jason said, "What's a honey bee, and how are you different from other types of bees?"

"Hold on there, boy! One question at a time, please," the bee replied.

"I'm sorry," Jason said. "I'm interested in what you do."

"There are other kinds of bees out here, but most of them don't live in a colony like I do." The honey bee seemed to be rather proud of this fact. "I'm here to collect some nectar and pollen for my colony, and I'm busy, so buzz off."

Jason decided to ignore the bee's attitude, and he introduced himself politely. "My name is Jason, Mr. Bee. "Could you please tell me what a colony is?"

The bee immediately stopped its collecting again and looked at Jason with great curiosity. "I am Miss Honey bee to you," she snapped, and she followed her comment with a few stretches of her body and wings.

"If you must know, a honey bee colony is a place where many of us live together, and we function as a team. And why do you ask so many questions?"

"Sorry. I promised Mrs. Grasshopper I would be more aware of things around me and learn from everyone I meet. I'm very interested in all the animals and plants out here." Jason then asked, "What did you mean when you said you worked as a team?"

"We have a queen, you see, and she lays all the eggs that will eventually become our young bees. That's mostly what she does, although she makes special chemicals in her body that help keep us all together. She also roams around the colony and checks to see if things are all functioning properly. She's very important to our well being.

"You may not know this but because she lays all the eggs, all of the other bees in the colony are related. Since we all have the same mother, the rest of us are all sisters. We are called workers, and we have a lot of other jobs in the colony."

"Wait, Miss Honey Bee, what do you mean, sisters? Aren't there any boys in your colony?"

"Oh, yes," the honey bee explained. "There are boys, but they don't do any work. We girls do all the work! The boys just mate with new queens that are produced in our colonies."

Jason asked, "What sorts of jobs do you have?"

"Some of us workers do what I'm doing right now so we can bring pollen and nectar back to our colony and feed the young and other adult bees that are working there."

"I don't really know exactly what pollen and nectar are," said Jason. "Could you explain it to me?"

"You sure ask a lot of questions," the honey bee said. "But since you have asked me these questions politely, I'll explain it to you. Pollen is very little powder-like things the flowers make, and when we bees drop some on flowers, they fertilize them, and they can make fruits and seeds. Much of the fruit you eat grows because we pollinate their plants. Nectar is a liquid made by plants which has different types of sugars in it, and we carry it back to our colonies to make honey from it. We need both pollen and nectar to stay alive."

Jason said, "That's very interesting, Miss Honey Bee. I can see that those jobs are very important. Are there other things that you bees do?"

"Why yes, there are. Some of the bees in our colony build cells of wax that we produce from special glands in our abdomen. Some take care of the young and clean the colony. Still others help produce new queens that will go out and start their own colonies."

"Isn't that a little strange," Jason asked, "making your own wax?"

Miss Honey Bee chides Jason. "No. Not at all! We use it to build with. All the cells within our colony are made of wax. We're not the only animals to make wax, you know. You humans make it in your ears, and you don't even use it to build anything."

"Okay, okay, I'm sorry," said Jason. "What are some of the other jobs you have?"

"Other bees in the colony specialize in removing water from the nectar that is brought in by other bees. The honey that results from this process can be stored in some of the colony's cells for later use. At certain times of the year, when plants are not producing nectar, like during the winter, we feed on the honey. It keeps us alive until the springtime comes, when we can go out and begin collecting nectar again."

View of underside of a honey bee, showing wax that has been produced from glands on its abdomen. They use the wax to build the cells in their hive, in which they store honey and raise their young.

Jason was beginning to realize that the honey bee was now talking without a break between her sentences. There was hardly enough time to ask questions.

"Collecting nectar and making honey is hard work, you know. It takes quite a few trips to flowers for us to get enough nectar to make even a little bit of honey. That's why we spend most of our time collecting it instead of talking to strange little boys!"

Jason smiled at the honey bee's sarcastic comment.

"Still other workers protect the colony if something tries to harm us. We can sting when we want to, but we only do that when we feel our colony is going to be harmed. As you can see, we have quite a system of team work going on. That's how we can build our colonies to be very large." Miss Honey Bee fanned her wings proudly.

Jason said, "You certainly do have excellent team work. There's no doubt about that. Are there any other insects that live like you do?"

"Well, yes." The honey bee thought for a moment. "There are other insects that live in colonies, but they're not exactly like us. Ants sometimes have very large colonies, but, of course, their workers can't fly. They're wingless. Only the female ants that will be queens and the males have wings.

"Certain wasps build nests of paper for their colonies to stay in. Termites often live in very large colonies. There are a few more types of wasps and bees that live in colonies as well, but most other insects don't have colonies at all."

Jason said, "Mrs. Grasshopper told me that everyone in this habitat has a role to play in helping to keep some sort of a balance. What sort of role do you have?"

Miss Honey Bee proudly answered, "Well, it's like I said. When we collect pollen, we help the plants by pollinating them. As you know, it's because of our pollination that they can make fruits and seeds. When the seeds fall to the ground or are planted by you humans, new plants sprout from them, and this makes more food for other animals.

"Humans even depend on us to pollinate things for them, like many of the farm crops and fruit trees. Of course, we get help from the wind and some other types of insects too. Some of the other insects that are especially important in pollination are certain flies, beetles, moths and ants, sometimes even butterflies and wasps."

Without as much as catching her breath, she continued. "Some humans which you call beekeepers set up special box-like houses for us to live in because they know how important we are at pollinating. Sometimes, they even move our houses around from crop to crop so we can pollinate different types of plants. In the process, we make lots of honey, and sometimes these beekeepers take some of it to use and sell at markets. It is a special kind of relationship we have with these humans, and we each benefit from it.

"The wax we make our colonies out of is very soft and is often used by humans to make a lot of things, like lipsticks and skin care products. So you see, without us, humans wouldn't have honey or our special wax, and many plants wouldn't get pollinated. It's easy to see that we are very important members of our community."

Jason was impressed with the importance of honey bees and said, "Wow! There's no doubt that you have many very important jobs here, Miss

Honey Bee. Do you have to worry about anything in particular in your environment?"

"Oh yes, we certainly do. Some things try to eat us, like spiders, certain other insects and birds, but our main problem is with pesticides. You see, Jason, when chemicals like pesticides are used in the field, they kill not only the insects that hurt plants, they often kill us too." Miss Honey Bee sadly shook her head.

"It upsets the balance that I heard you and Mrs. Grasshopper talking about. It's true that pesticides keep a lot of insects from eating the plants, but without us, there wouldn't be very many plants. It's a very important thing to think about."

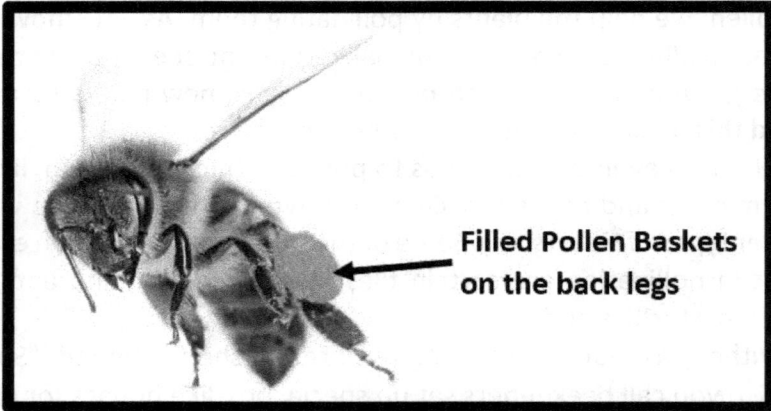

Filled Pollen Baskets on the back legs

A honey bee worker with its pollen baskets on its hind legs filled with pollen. Honey bees obtain protein in their diet by eating pollen. In the process of collecting it, they pollenate the flowers they visit. They obtain sugars from the nectar they feed upon. The honey we eat is made from nectar that was, at one time, stored in a honey bee hive.

Jason considered what Miss Honey Bee said and vowed, "I'll try to tell everyone to be very careful about using pesticides. You can bet on that. Thanks for talking with me, Miss Honey Bee. I learned a lot from our conversation. Keep up the good work. Now I know why people say, "Busy as a bee."

As Jason waved goodbye, the honey bee began moving its wings for flight, but it seemed to have trouble lifting off the flower because of its heavy pollen load. With great effort, it finally became airborne. Jason waved another goodbye and began to concentrate on other things in his surroundings.

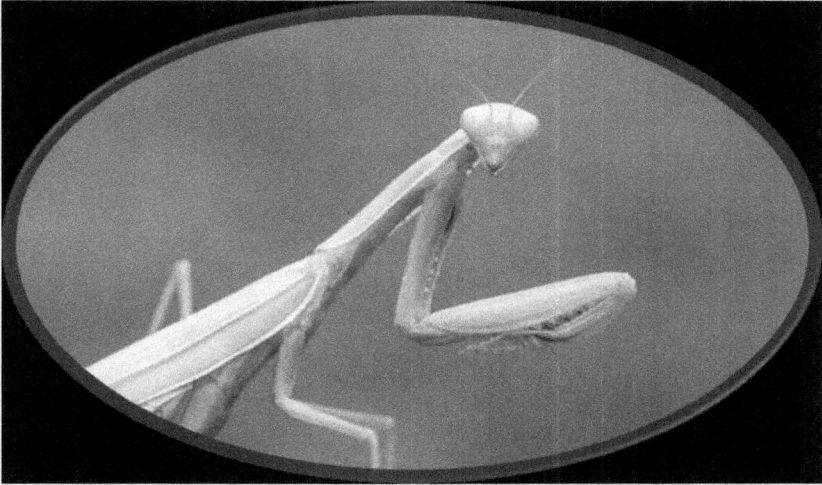

⑧

The Praying Mantid

As he looked down toward the middle of the plant nearest him, Jason saw what had formerly appeared to be tiny aphids, sucking juice from the plant's stem. Seeing them reminded him of the time he had first seen them in his garden in the city, but this time they were half his size. Suddenly, a ladybird beetle that appeared to be the size of a small car came his way, eating aphids as it moved along. He thought about how the ladybird beetle was actually helping the plant by eating insects that could cause the plant some harm.

Being a little more at ease in the field, he said, "Hello." to the ladybird beetle, but the insect appeared to be too busy with devouring aphids to hear him. It was making a loud munching sound with its chewing, and one after one, it downed the plant's pests. Jason could see that the beetle was much too busy to talk to him, so after watching for a minute or two, he began to look around at other spots on the plant.

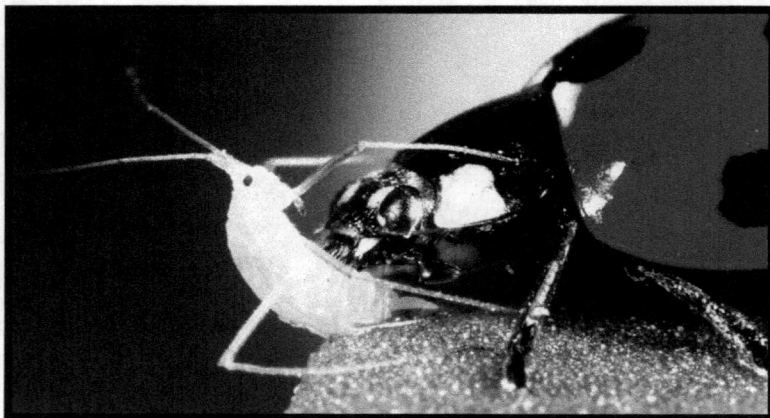

A ladybird beetle (right) eating an aphid. Because they feed on insects that harm plants, ladybird beetles are often referred to as beneficial insects.

As he looked down toward the ground, he saw other types of insects walking on the soil. Some of them seemed to leisurely walk over the surface while others scurried by, apparently searching for something. Some were even catching other insects and eating them.

David also had told him that some insects even spent much of their time underground, feeding on the plants' roots. He was amazed at the tremendous variety of these creatures and the various ways in which they interacted with one another.

As he stood up and peered toward the sky, he suddenly saw an unusual movement near a flower head. He then focused on what turned out to be a long and slender insect which was apparently resting near the top of the plant. While he watched, he couldn't get over the large size of its bulging eyes and how it turned its head almost completely around. It obviously had very good vision. As he studied it closely, it suddenly reeled its head downward, looked directly at him, and spoke. "How are you, boy? Are you having a nice field trip?"

Mantid, showing how it holds its raptorial (grabbing) forelegs with which it catches other insects.

"Yes, I am," said Jason, "but how do you know I'm on a field trip?"

"Because I've been watching you for a while." said the insect. "I watch everything out here in the field."

Jason asked, "What are you, anyway?"

"I'm called a praying mantid or mantis, although I'm not really praying. This is how I hold my front legs, and it just looks like I'm praying. I use my front legs to grab things with."

"I do remember seeing someone like you before," Jason said. "What do you do?"

"I look around for other insects. When I see one, I quickly snatch it up, and then I eat it. I usually get my best meals out here in the field."

"Well, that's not very nice, eating your own kind. Couldn't you do something else?"

"No, not really. That's what I do. I'm the next step in the food chain from the insects that you've been talking to."

Jason said, "I'm not sure about what you mean by food chain. Could you explain this to me?"

"Well," the mantid said, "let's take it from the beginning so you can understand the big picture. Plants grow and produce their own food by getting energy from the sun. I hope you know that."

"Why, yes, I do." said Jason. "I know that is an important thing for plants to do, but I have a feeling that there's more to it than that."

Plant ⟶ Herbivore ⟶ Predator ⟶ Other Predators

A short food chain. Plants receive energy from the sun. When an herbivore eats the plant, the energy is passed on to it, and when a predator eats the herbivore, the energy is passed on to it as well. Energy like this flows through all members of a community.

"You're absolutely right," the mantid remarked. "Have a little patience, boy. I'll get to the rest of the story. You see, certain insects eat the plants, and then someone like me comes along and eats them. Then, unfortunately for us mantids, there's someone who will try to eat me. It's a chain-like reaction in nature, and it contributes to the balance I've been hearing you talk about. It's a very important concept.

"I'm different from most of the other insects out here, you see, just like you're different from a cow or a pig. You eat them, and you don't see me getting all huffy because of it. I catch my meals with my specially-developed front legs, and my mouthparts are made for eating things of that type.

"When I become an adult and have enough to eat, I mate and lay eggs that usually hatch the following year, after the winter is over. If I didn't have the other insects to eat, I would starve to death, and I wouldn't be able to have children."

"I'm sorry I didn't appreciate you when we first met. I'm sure you're important in this habitat."

"You bet I am. If I didn't eat a lot of these insects, their populations would get very large, and many of them would eat the plants until they had no leaves left. Without leaves, the plants wouldn't be able to make their food, and we'd all be in trouble. You see, when they make their food, they produce oxygen, and that's what all animals breathe, including you humans. Without oxygen, we'd all die."

Jason said, "I guess you have a similar role in the balance out here to the ladybird beetle, don't you?"

"Why, yes, I do. I'm impressed that you noticed the similarity between us. There is a difference though. We eat different insects. It eats small ones, and I eat larger ones, so we both help the plant but in different ways. Together, we're partly responsible for the plant's health."

"Wow!" said Jason, "That's a pretty big responsibility. What about enemies? Do you have any particular ones out here in the field?"

"Oh, yes," said the mantid. "We have many kinds of enemies, like birds and spiders. Sometimes other mantids even attempt to eat us. We have to be very careful out here.

"Maybe you've noticed that mantids are either light green or light brown in color. Those colors help us to blend in with the surrounding plants. By blending in, the birds and other predators can't see us as well. Some types of mantids, especially in tropical areas of the world, have parts of their body that look exactly like leaves and other parts of plants."

"I can see how that works," Jason said. "I've seen other insects that were colored like you, but there are some insects that have bright colors. How does that work?"

"That's a very interesting question," the mantid said. "Those insects with bright colors usually can hurt something that's trying to eat them, and the bright colors represent a type of warning that tells predators to stay away or something unpleasant will happen."

Jason asked, "What unpleasant things can happen?"

"Well, the insect could have unpleasant or poisonous chemicals in its body that can hurt and possibly even kill a bird or other predator that eats them. Predators, you know, are animals like me that eat other animals."

"Yes, I know that. But what good is poisoning the bird after it eats the insect?"

"That's another very good question," said the mantid. "If the predator detects an unpleasant taste, it sometimes will spit the insect out right away, and the insect goes about its business without harm to its body. At times when a bird actually eats the insect, the predator may get sick, and it will remember not to eat another one. Protection is then afforded to insects just like it and other insects that look like it.

"After the bird eats the insect and gets sick from eating it, it probably will never eat another one of that type in its entire life. That also means that other insects that look like it gain protection from the bird's bad experience with trying to eat one of them. Somehow, adult birds even teach each other and their young about these things. It's a very complex situation that some other insects take advantage of."

Jason asked, "What do you mean?"

"It works like this. Some insects mimic other insects, and by doing this their species gains protection from their being eaten. They may be shaped like the insects that they are mimicking, and they may even have the same patterns and colors in their body that the other insects have. When a bird learns not to eat something with those shapes, patterns and colors, they won't eat the mimics either."

Jason asked, "Are there other ways that the insects with bright colors could hurt something that's going to eat them?"

"Oh yes, there are. Some insects sting and some bite, like bees, ants, wasps, and some caterpillars. Some spray irritating chemicals on animals that are going to eat them, like certain ants and beetles. There are many ways that insects defend themselves."

"Wow, that's bizarre," said Jason. "I'll have to watch out for these things. I had no idea that such complex things were going on out here. Thanks for all the information, and good luck to you."

There are many forms of mimics. This spider has a body structure similar to a very venomous type of ant. Mimics often fool potential predators into thinking they are dangerous and should not be approached. Thus, it is a way of staying alive.

"And good luck to you, boy, and thank you for asking about us. Most people don't seem to care much about us.

"Before you go, I'd like to make a recommendation. If you have a chance to talk to a possum during your field trip, ask her about these things. She seems to know quite a bit about how different animals defend them-selves. And while you're out there, say hello to the other animals when you get a chance."

⑨

The Millipede

As Jason watched, the mantid carefully leaned toward a fly that had landed on the top of the plant. Quicker than the eye could see, it seized it and began eating away as though it was the most delicious food it had ever put its mouthparts on.

Not wanting to bother the mantid during its meal, Jason looked toward the ground and noticed something very long and round crawling on the soil by his feet. It was very unusual because it had more legs than most things he'd ever seen.

As he watched it moving over the ground, he wondered how the animal could ever keep all its legs working together. He only had two, and he

51

sometimes stumbled over them. As the animal moved, its legs appeared to have a rippling motion.

Jason stooped down to get a closer look, and the creature suddenly grew to an enormous size. Now standing as its equal, Jason said, "Who are you? I'm not sure I've seen you before."

"I'm a millipede, and I see you're a human."

"Why, yes, I am," said Jason. "Are you one of those insects we humans call a thousand-legger?"

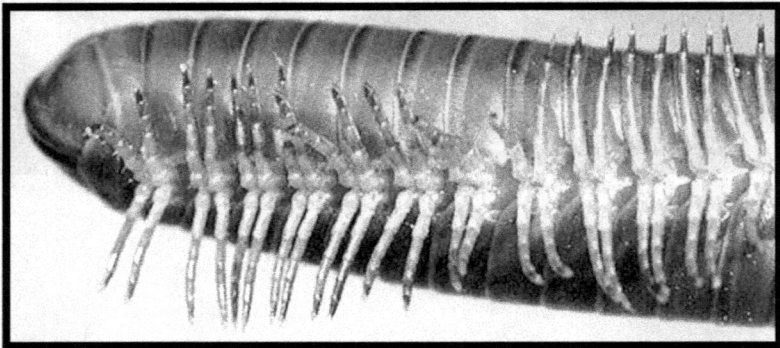

Millipede legs, showing their rhythm of movement when walking. These movements are guided by their nervous system so they don't have to think about the process.

"First of all," said the millipede, "I'm not an insect at all. Insects have six legs and three body regions. As you can see, I have many legs and many body segments, all in a row. Secondly, you humans named me. The word millipede means a thousand feet, but, of course, we never have as many as that. Most of us have at least thirty pairs of legs though."

Jason said, "You look something like a centipede. Are you related to them?"

"Oh no, we're not. There are many important differences between us. For instance, their bodies are usually flat, while ours are usually more round. There are exceptions, though. They also have their first pair of legs modified into devices that function as venom fangs, but we have no fangs.

"Centipedes are what you humans call predators, which means they catch and eat other live animals. We millipedes feed mostly on algae and decomposing plant materials."

Jason said, "Mantids are predators, too. I just talked to one a few minutes ago."

"Yes, they are predators," said the millipede, "but they eat living things up above the ground while centipedes generally eat things on the ground. I might remind you, though, that you're talking to me, a millipede, and I don't do anything like that."

Jason said, "If you can't bite, do you sting?"

"No, I don't," said the millipede.

"Well," said Jason, "if you can't bite or sting, how do you protect yourself from predators, whoever they are?"

"Many of us can roll up into a ball, and it's difficult for predators to hurt us when we're like that. Of course, a bird sometimes can get hold of us. Also, we sometimes have warning colors that tell predators to stay away from us. I think the mantid was telling you about that a minute ago."

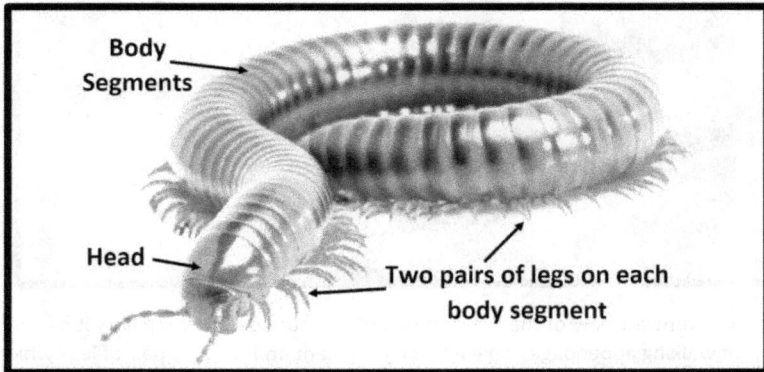

Millipedes are generally round. Many are small, about an inch or so long, while others, such as some African species, get to be almost a foot long. While centipedes have a single pair of legs on each of their body segments, millipedes have two pairs.

"But what happens if something tries to eat you anyway, like this bird you just mentioned?"

"I think the mantid was right, boy. You're a little impatient when it comes to listening to us. You need to slow down a little."

"I'm just very interested in learning about you and all the other animals out here," Jason commented. "I apologize."

"Oh, that's alright. I'm just kidding you anyway. To answer your question, we have special glands in our bodies that produce poisonous gases and other types of unpleasant chemicals. Once a predator gets a whiff of them, it's not likely to continue to prey on us."

Jason said, "I'm still a little confused. If I were to find something that looks like you, how would I tell if you were a centipede or a millipede?"

"It's very easy once you know how. We both have long bodies with many segments, but what you need to do is look at the relationship between our body segments and legs. We millipedes have two pairs of legs on each body segment while centipedes have only one pair on each segment. Also, we tend to walk a lot slower than centipedes.

Bottom (ventral) view of the anterior end of a centipede, showing how it has one pair of walking appendages on each body segment and the first pair of legs which have developed into venom-delivering fangs (arrow). Millipedes do not have such fangs.

"You may have to use a magnifying glass to determine the number of legs on each segment, especially on the little ones, but please be careful. Use a pair of forceps when handling something you don't know about. A centipede can sometimes give you a serious bite."

"Thanks for the advice." Jason was especially thankful for this advice because one thing he didn't need was a venomous bite.

"I don't understand how you fit in with all the other creatures to help in the balance out here in nature. Can you tell me something about that?"

"Sure, I'd be happy to tell you," said the millipede. "It's not always easy to see what one animal does that fits in with nature, but we all have our roles.

"We millipedes crawl upon the ground, sometimes eating plant material, and sometimes doing other things, like mating and depositing eggs. In crawling around, we often pick up spores and seeds from plants, and we help distribute them to other areas."

All of a sudden, Jason seemed confused. "I know what seeds are, but what are spores?"

"Well, spores are very tiny particles that are given off by some plants or plant-like organisms, like fungus, mosses, and ferns. They are much smaller than seeds, but they are like seeds in a way because plants grow from them when the conditions are right."

Jason said, "Thanks for clearing that up."

The millipede continued. "Also, we function in the food chain by cleaning up decomposing materials. There are larger animals that you know of that do this, like vultures, some birds of prey, possums, rodents, dogs, cats, and others. There also are many kinds of insects that do this, as well as bacteria and other small living things.

"We, just like them, help return nutrients from dead things back to the environment. That way, bacteria and other very small living things can feed on them and change them into chemicals that plants can use again. What we do is a very important part of nature."

Jason said, "I never would have guessed that your role in nature is so important. Thank you for doing your job and explaining it to me, and good luck."

"The pleasure is all mine," said the millipede. "Good luck on your field trip."

⑩

The Sparrow

I t wasn't because Jason was bored with the lives of insects and other animals around him that caused him to look toward the sky. It was the sudden shadows of birds flying overhead and their chattering that drew his
attention upward.

He saw a number of buzzards circling very high overhead, floating on
the updrafts of summer winds, flocks of crows squawking back and forth
about something or other, and an invasion of smaller birds that landed
nearby. He listened to the excitement as the birds found and competed for
the food that they had been looking for.

Just as he was in the process of standing, alternating from being flat-footed on the ground to stretching to a tip-toed stance to see above the vegetation, a bird landed on the plant by his head. As they stared at one another, the bird suddenly became larger and said, "Hello, young man. I see you're examining things around you very closely. What are you doing out here in an open field?"

"I'm studying animals out here, and I find it very interesting. Just a minute ago, I was talking to a millipede. How about you? Are you out here for a particular reason?"

"Yes, I am," the bird answered. "I'm here to find some seeds. You see, that's what I eat mostly. Some of my friends told me about those millipedes. They don't taste very good is what I've heard."

Jason said, "My name is Jason. Who are you?"

"I'm a sparrow. I come out here often with my friends. Lately, I've been trying to eat a little more because I have young birds to feed."

Jason said, "It's nice to hear that you have a family. I hope they are doing well."

"Yes, they are. Thank you."

"You said you eat mostly seeds. What else do you eat?"

"I eat occasional insects and things similar to insects, like spiders, but they're usually small. I've never tried to eat a millipede, though. Some of my bird relatives, like mocking birds and robins, eat larger things, sometimes even worms. When you think of birds as one big group, you'll find that we eat most anything."

"Like what?" Jason asked, becoming more interested.

"Well, there are hawks, eagles, and owls that catch other animals. There are some birds, like secretary birds in Africa, that even specialize in eating snakes. There are some local kinds of birds, like shrikes, that eat lots of lizards. Then, there are the buzzards who specialize in eating dead things. Sometimes you can look at our beak or feet and tell what we eat and do."

"That sounds very interesting. How about giving me some examples," Jason said.

"Okay. When you look at an eagle's beak, it's easy to see that it is very strong and hooked at the end. You can tell it's made for tearing into flesh. Their feet are large for grasping, and their claws are large and sharp. These things are necessary for catching animals. Hawks, falcons, and kites

57

have similar beaks and feet, so you know they're predators of some sort."

An eagle with a strong, pointed, and hooked beak, characteristic of birds that prey on other animals. Bald eagles feed mostly on fish. Other predatory birds may feed on other types of animals. All such predatory birds have very acute vision to see their prey.

"Are there any other features that stand out in a predatory bird?" Jason questioned.

"Why yes, there are. Those types of birds also have very good vision so they can spot their prey from great distances, and they can fly very fast. When they spot their prey, which on land is usually a rabbit, a rodent, or a snake, they swoop down and attempt to grab it or knock it down before it has a chance to get to safety."

"What other types of birds are there?" Jason asked.

"Woodpeckers have a long, slender beak, and their feet are different from those of most birds. Their beaks are slender to go into holes and they even sometimes make holes in trees. Their tongue is very long, and when they stick their beaks into holes, their tongue goes even deeper to catch insects that may be hiding there, and they may also drink the sap that leaks from the holes.

"Their feet have two toes on the front and two on the back to help them climb around on the tree. There aren't many birds that have feet like that. Another group with similar feet is the parrots, but their beak is much different. They feed mostly on plants and large seeds, and they sometimes use their beaks to rip fruit apart.

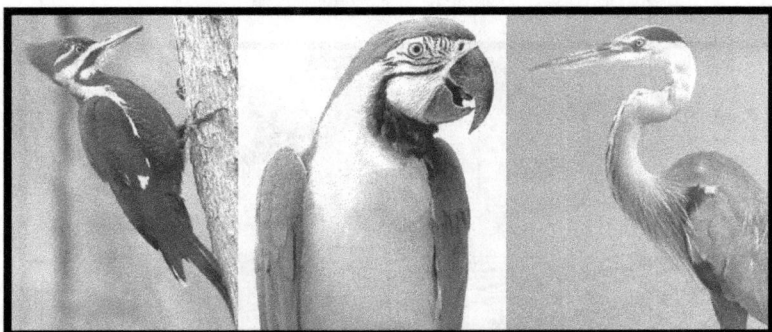

Birds with different beaks. The pileated woodpecker on the left has a long slender beak with which it withdraws insects from the tissues of a tree. Parrots (center), on the other hand have a beak with which it can tear into wood and fruit. The great blue heron on the right has a long slender beak with which it catches fish and other animals that are found around water.

"Although both woodpeckers and parrots nest in tree holes, and they use their beaks to make the holes, they use them in other ways, as well. Woodpeckers use their beaks like an ax to chop into the wood, while parrots use their beaks to tear and scrape the wood," the sparrow explained slowly.

Jason said, "There sure are a lot of ways that birds use their beaks and feet. What about you?"

"Well, my beak is small and straight, so I can't tear with it or dig holes. That's why I eat mostly seeds and small insects. There are some small birds, like finches, that have thicker beaks than mine, which help them crack seeds open better than we can.

"There are many more types of beaks and feet in the bird world. Herons, egrets and some other wading birds, for instance, have long, slender beaks to catch fish with. Their feet usually spread out when they move so they can walk on vegetation that floats on or near the top of the water or on the soft mud at the bottom of a pond.

"As you know, ducks and similar birds that swim a lot have webbed feet to help them move through the water. Their beaks are designed for sifting through plant materials. Is there anything else you want to know about us birds?"

Jason said, "Wow! You've told me a lot already, but I do have a few more questions about other things. You mentioned nesting in holes by woodpeckers and parrots. Birds nest in other ways too, don't they?"

Bird's nest. Most small birds construct a nest with twigs and grass in the forks of branches, making a bed by putting feathers on top of the larger parts. Woodpeckers and parrots make a hole in trees and lay their eggs inside. Ducks, seagulls, whipoorwills, killdeer, and certain other birds deposit their eggs in shallow, poorly-defined nests on the ground. Eagles and other large birds may build their nest high in trees or on the sides of cliffs, using mostly tree branches and twigs and lining them with feathers and other soft materials.

"Oh, yes," agreed the sparrow, happy that Jason was so interested in what was being said. "When sparrows and many other small birds nest, they gather mostly grass, string and other soft materials and build a nest in the shape of a bowl. We line our nests with even softer materials, like feathers. By doing that, it's nice and soft for our young ones, and it helps insulate the eggs and young from changing temperatures.

"Large birds, like eagles and hawks, usually build a nest with twigs and branches, but they often put softer materials inside for their young to be on, as well. Their nests are usually high up in trees or on the sides of rock cliffs where it's safe from other predators.

"Some smaller birds, like orioles and certain finches, build hanging nests, and they have to weave grasses together so the nest will hang properly and not fall. Then, there are other types of birds, like killdeer, night hawks, gulls, and terns, that don't use plant parts at all to make their nest. They usually make a slight depression in the ground and lay their eggs in the depression."

Jason shook his head slowly and said, "Wow! There is a lot about birds I didn't know. Before you go, I'd like to know how you fit into this habitat with the other animals."

"Actually," the sparrow said, "we're not restricted to this habitat like some of the other animals are. Since we have wings and fly very well, we can fly to different habitats. Sometimes we'll stay in the woodlands during the heat of the day and come out to eat in the fields in the mornings and evenings. Different birds do different things, of course. There are even some, like night herons, night hawks, and owls that are active at night.

"To answer your question, when we eat seeds, we sometimes drop some, and they fall to the ground and sprout. This helps spread the plants from place to place. Sometimes we eat the seeds, and they pass through our bodies, only to be deposited later when they pass out.

"To repeat a little of what I've said, woodpeckers and many other birds eat insects; eagles, hawks, falcons, and kites eat other animals; herons, egrets, anhingas, and cormorants eat fish and sometimes lizards, frogs, and small snakes; ducks, coots, and gallinules eat vegetation in and around the water. By eating so many different things, we help the environment.

"If you think about it, you'll realize that we're part of the balance in nature, just like any of the other animals in nature. Unfortunately, there are many things that can eat us. There are weasels and other aquatic animals, foxes, cats, dogs, snakes, and other land animals that sometimes catch us, and humans have been known to eat us too. It's a very difficult world to deal with sometimes out here in nature."

"Well, I won't take up more of your time," Jason said. "I really appreciate what you're doing out here, and I hope to see you again. Good luck with your family."

"Thanks," said the sparrow. "Énjoy your day."

⑪

The Blue Racer

As he approached the woodland edge, Jason couldn't help but notice periodic movement out of the corner of his eye, but when he looked toward it, he saw nothing but what appeared to be plants, scattered twigs, and logs. Wanting to discover what it was that was attracting his attention, he slowly and carefully edged forward in the direction of the movement, watching that he didn't step on a twig and frighten whatever it was away.

He stopped abruptly when he noticed a rather long, slender bluish-brown snake on top of a stump directly in front of him. By the time he was aware of what it was, he was close enough to notice the snake had a black patch over its eye area and a lighter colored underside. The patch reminded him of the mask worn by a bandit or one of the western heroes in old movies he had seen.

He realized why he hadn't recognized it when he looked in that direction. Its color was drab, and it blended in very well with other things in the environment. It was a form of camouflage, he thought, just as the mantid explained when talking about insects that blended in with their environment, and the manner in which it remained still most of the time helped keep it hidden, even when it was out in the open.

Since he knew nothing about the snake, he was a little cautious and decided it would be best to remain still and study the situation before going closer. In the meantime, it appeared that the snake was watching him too. As they stared at one another, the snake grew to an enormous size, flicked out its forked tongue several times, and finally said, "You don't have to be afraid of me, boy. I'm a blue racer, and I don't hurt people."

"But, but you do bite, don't you? And don't you chase people?"

"Hogwash," the blue racer said. "As snakes go, I do move very fast, and when I'm trying to get away from danger, I may accidentally run towards someone, but I don't run after them. I'll let you in on a little secret. I'm just as afraid of them as they are of me.

"Relax. I can see you're out here to learn about all the animals, and I know you respect us for what we are. We're animals just like anything else out here, including you.

"Now, if someone tries to catch me, I will try to bite them, and I am very quick about it, but you would do the same if some giant came up to you and tried to catch you.

"Even if I did bite, it wouldn't hurt you much. I'm not venomouse. Some of my relatives are though, like rattlesnakes, moccasins, copperheads, and coral snakes, but I'm harmless.

"It is true that I have a lot of teeth, and they're very sharp. In fact, I have six rows of teeth, four rows above and two below. They help me hold on to my food when I eat, but they're very small and pin-like."

"I'm a little confused," said Jason. "You call yourself a blue racer, but you're bluish-brown. Why aren't you a brown racer?"

"That's a very good question," said the blue racer. "I guess you could call me a brown racer if you like, or just a racer for short.

"You see, we are found in many different places throughout the country, and we have different colors in different parts of our range. Some of my species are somewhat blue in color, and that's why we, as a group, are referred to as blue racers.

"Of course, there are some of us in other parts of the country that are even greenish, and some of the local people call us green racers. I know it's a little confusing, but you humans are the ones who named us."

Jason asked, "What type of animals are snakes, anyway? What is a blue racer?"

"We blue racers are snakes, as you have just said, and snakes are reptiles. Examples of other types of reptiles are alligators, crocodiles, turtles, and lizards. The one thing all of the reptiles have in common is a scaly skin.

"We reptiles that are on the earth today have had distant relatives who lived many millions of years ago when reptiles ruled the earth. They are called dinosaurs, and some of them got very large. I think you humans find that group of reptiles very interesting, isn't that true?"

"Yes," said Jason. "They are a popular group of animals. I really enjoy it when we go to museums and see the skeletons of those animals. It must have been an interesting time on earth when they existed."

"Oh, it was," said the blue racer. "Of course, we blue racers didn't exist back then, and neither did humans. Today's snakes don't really get very large when compared to the reptiles that existed during the realm of the dinosaurs. The largest snakes today, like the pythons, anacondas, and boas of Africa and South America, are, at most, about thirty feet in length. The biggest snakes in the United States are about eight or nine feet long."

Jason said, "That's plenty big for me. Tell me something, though. Many of my friends in the city say that you snakes are slimy. Is that true?"

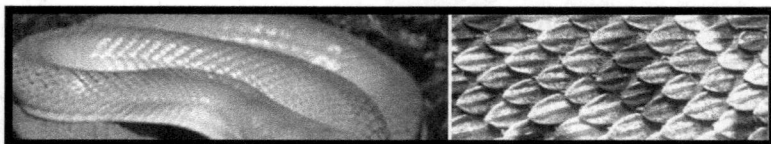

Scales of snakes. On the left are the smooth scales of a non-venous green snake. On the right are the rough scales of a rattlesnake. Raptile scales are made of keratin, the same type of chemical that is in our skin.

"Of course we're not. Why would we be slimy? We have no body secretions that would make us that way. In fact, we have very dry skin. The texture of our skin can be smooth or rough, depending on the types of scales we have on our body. My body is very smooth, but the skin of a water snake is quite rough. Run your hand over my scales and see for yourself."

Jason reached over, touched the snake, and ran his hand down his back. It was true. The blue racer's scales were very smooth, and his body was soft and warm.

"Now, if you see snakes in the water, they may be wet and slippery, but we're not slimy. If you choose to use the term 'slimy' at all for describing animals, it's the worms, snails, slugs, and fish that are slimy. They have secretions in their skin that make them slimy to the touch."

"I couldn't help but notice that when I put my hand on your body, it was warm. I thought all you snakes were cold blooded."

"Well, you'll find that the term 'cold blooded' isn't used much anymore, and for good reason. You see, our bodies are cold when the temperature in our environment is cold, but when we have a chance to lay out in the sun, we pick up some of its radiant heat, and our body becomes warm. We have to be careful, though, because if we lay out in the sun too long, we can overheat. We just can't produce a body heat like you humans can."

Jason said, "Oh, I see." Then he asked, "As a reptile, what do you do here?"

"Well, let's see. I slither around, try to lay out in the sun in the mornings to warm up my body, and I catch things to eat. I was beginning to take a nap when you startled me."

Jason said, "I'm very sorry for awakening you, but it looked to me like you were wide awake when I first saw you. How could you be sleeping?'

"I'm just like all other snakes in not having eyelids. My eyes are always open. That's one way to tell us snakes from legless and other types of lizards. Most lizards have eyelids and can close their eyes when they sleep. Of course, there are some lizards that don't have eyelids, like geckos."

This was very curious to Jason. He wondered how it would be to always have his eyes open. He couldn't see how it was possible to get a good night's sleep like that.

Another question suddenly popped into his mind, based on what the snake had just said. "You mentioned legless lizards. I didn't know there were such things."

"Oh yes," the snake said. "There are several types that look like

65

snakes. They are most common in the warmer parts of the country."

"What kind of things do you eat out here in nature, snake? Do you eat insects and things like that?"

Small snakes. Left, a ringneck snake is blackish with a yellow or orange ring of scales around its neck. Right, a very secretive worm snake (named such because it looks like a worm) is among the smallest snakes in the world.

"I eat a lot of things that exist here, like mice, lizards, occasional frogs, and a bird once in a while. Some of my relatives, like the slender green snakes, eat insects once in a while, but they eat frogs too. Ringneck snakes and many of the other small types of snakes even eat worms, but they're not to my liking. When you consider snakes as a whole, we eat just about anything in nature that you can think of except plants.

Jason asked, "What else do you do here?"

"I crawl around a lot. Believe it or not, I move by walking on my ribs. I know that may seem a little odd to you, but I don't have arms and legs to move around with. Most reptiles other than snakes have legs.

"Of course, there are exceptions. The legless lizards I mentioned before more-or-less move like we do.

"Getting back to moving, when I crawl, my ribs move something like the legs of a millipede or centipede. I don't really think about it. That's just how they do. I don't think you think much about how you move, do you?"

"No, I don't," said Jason.

It appeared to Jason that the blue racer was on a roll and wanted to talk as long as he was willing to listen.

"Once in a while," he said, "I shed my skin. All reptiles do this, but when snakes do it, our skin usually comes off in one big piece. We even shed the skin over our eyes.

"Most other reptiles shed their skin in smaller pieces. When you're out looking at animals sometime, talk to a lizard, and they'll tell you how they do it.

"Other animals shed their skin, too, even humans."

Jason was surprised at the blue racer's comment. He never thought of himself as an animal that shed its skin, so he said, "I don't remember shedding. Are you sure about this?"

"It's not something you'd really know about because you humans take baths and showers all the time, and your dead skin comes off when you wash. It's easier to see the shed skin on your head, you know, that flaky stuff you call dandruff. Your skin has cells that keep producing new, living skin cells all the time. Those cells die and cover the living ones."

"I didn't know that." said Jason.

Without missing a beat, the blue racer continued. "Then I sometimes find a mate and lay eggs in a safe, moist place before the warm season is over. If my eggs are in a spot that's too dry, they will shrivel up and die, and if they are too wet, they will get moldy and die, so it's up to me to lay them in the right place. Most snakes that lay eggs do the same."

A rotting log is a good place to find snake eggs in nature. They thrive in dark, moist places.

"Is there anything that you're scared of here in nature?"

"Oh, yes. There are some things that can catch me, like raccoons, otters, and hawks. Sometimes, other snakes try to eat me. There's a king snake around here sometime, so I have to be very careful not to go by him."

Suddenly, the blue racer appeared startled. It quit talking and turned its head to the left, flicking out its tongue in the process. After a moment, he said, "I hate to break up our conversation, but I saw a few lizards moving around over by that other log, and I'm very hungry. I'll have to talk to you at another time."

"Okay, I won't bother you any longer." said Jason. "Thanks for talking to me. Keep taking in that sun, and be happy."

"I will. Say hello to the other animals when you see them." The words were no sooner out of his mouth when he slithered off the stump and gracefully moved in the direction of his potential food. Jason saw him last when his tail vanished beneath a log.

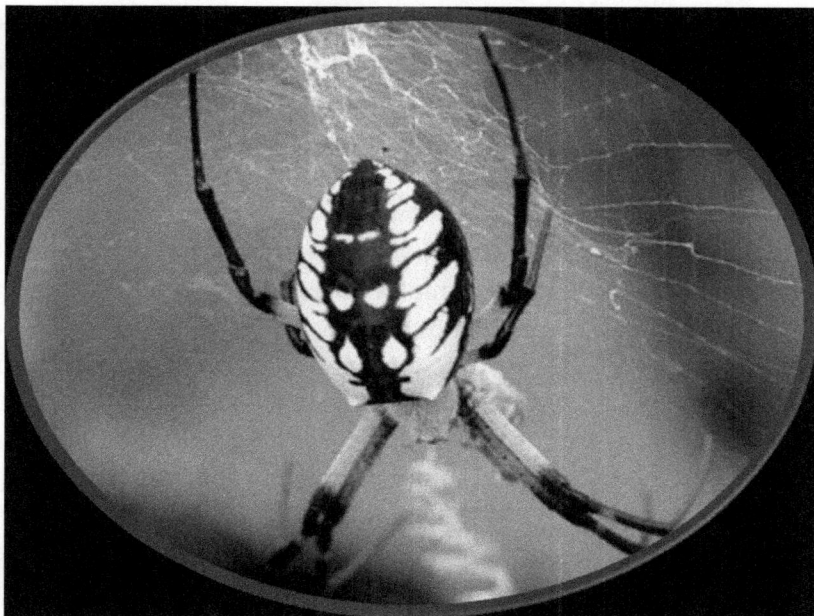

⑫

The Spider

As Jason exited from the field and walked along the woodland edge, he noticed logs everywhere. The trees had been drastically cut a year or two earlier, and many of them had been left to rot. He wondered what animals had suffered because their habitat was destroyed.

There were only straggly trees left, and vegetation not usually found in a forest had invaded the area. The land had not had a chance to progress very much toward the stage of being a new forest, and Jason knew that it would take many more years before that would happen.

It obviously had at one time been part of the woodland habitat that he was approaching. Yet, it was no longer suitable for woodland animals, and it wasn't quite appropriate for field-loving animals either. It appeared to be a link between the two.

As he rummaged around, rolling logs to look beneath them, he ran into a multitude of insects and similar small creatures that were often found in places like that. He found a few small snakes, like ring-necked and ground snakes, and nests that rodents had built.

Ants of many different sizes were abundant everywhere he looked, many of which had built nests within or under the logs. As he rolled the logs, many of the ants scattered, simultaneously picking up their young and attempting to carry them to safety. Understanding that he was upsetting their home, he limited his rolling to just a few logs.

With this same thought in mind, Jason rolled the logs back into their original spot just as David had told him to do when he finished examining the creatures that lived beneath them. He knew that leaving the log in a new position would cause many of the inhabitants to die or be forced to move to a more suitable location.

As he continued to examine this area, he noticed there were occasional spiders that had built small, funnel-shaped webs at the edge of many of the logs, and as he quietly sat and watched, they occasionally darted out to catch insects that crawled by. There was a myriad of other creatures that he didn't recognize, and when he attempted to get their attention, they scurried to hidden places.

When he finished rolling and replacing logs at the woodland edge, he realized that this was actually a type of habitat in itself, and many of the living things he found here probably wouldn't be found in other habitats. They specialized in living in the woodland edge or in disturbed habitats. Whoever logged this area had destroyed the habitat for some animals but unknowingly had provided the base for a new habitat and all of the animals that went along with it.

He also imagined that the woodland edge habitat would change over time. When the logs were initially cut, they were fresh and didn't provide an environment suitable for many of the critters that would eventually live there.

As logs rotted, many insects, like sawflies and certain beetles, invaded the changing habitat, laid their eggs in and on the wood, ate the wood and sought shelter beneath the decomposing material. Types of fungus, like mushrooms, and bacteria, assisted the decomposition process. Eventually, new kinds of plants became established, choking out the earlier vegetation. Other things that fed on them finally invaded the habitat, and eventually the bark loosened on the rotting logs and provided yet another place for creatures of all sorts to hide, feed and reproduce.

One example of a microhabitat is found here in bull horn acacia plants (a type of tropical plant) in which ants nest in the thorns (arrow to right). Instead of using nectar from flowers as part of their food, the ants use nectar from extrafloral nectaries (arrow on the left).

Suddenly, it dawned on him. You didn't have to look at large areas like a woodland, woodland edge, or field as the only habitats. Everywhere you looked, there were small habitats, ones David had called microhabitats, providing the needs of every conceivable type of creature, and each of these microhabitats had food chains of their own.

It could be under a log, in a log, in certain plants, high up in trees, almost anywhere, and they would change, depending on the type of large habitat they lived in. For instance, he thought, a pinewoods habitat would provide different things from one made up of hardwoods, like oaks. A warm environment would be different from a colder one. There were so many conditions that differed around the world, the number of different microhabitats would be astonishingly high. Jason recognized this as one of his most inspiring thoughts.

When he stood just inside the woodland habitat, he noticed very few small plants growing amongst the trees as compared to the vegetation of the field and woodland edge. The trees' canopy was largely blocking the sun from getting to the forest floor. Based on his earlier field trip with David, he instinctively knew this area also was going to be quite different in terms of the animals he found.

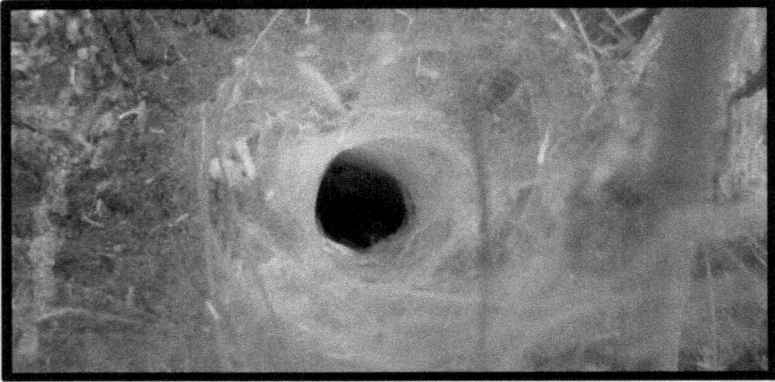

A funnel shaped web made by a spider that lives in a grassy environment. They wait until an insect comes close and then rush out and grab it. Spiders that construct a web that is hooked to plant material above the ground construct their web and wait for insects to get caught in it.

He was hardly into the woodland when all of a sudden, he ran into a huge spider web that had been constructed between two pine trees so that it hung over a barely noticeable path. He jumped back, the web clinging to his face, arms and clothes like ultra-thin slivers of highly elastic, sticky tape. As he pulled the sticky strands from his face and clothes and looked at the web from which they came, he noticed it had been constructed with a spiral-like circular arrangement, and near the center of the spiraling circles was a very large black and yellow spider, its legs stretched to hold onto the web. In a matter of seconds, it grew to an even larger size.

As Jason admired the interesting pattern on its body, he settled down from the scare he had had and asked, "Are you a dangerous spider?"

The spider turned to face Jason and answered, "No, not really. I'm an orb weaver. It does scare people when they run into my web, but I hardly ever bite large animals. Even when I do, it's because my life is threatened and I'm scared, but it really doesn't hurt that much.

"I build these webs across paths through the woods so I can trap insects when they fly through. That's what I eat. My web is made of silk that I make in my body, and when I finish constructing my web, it's like a giant net."

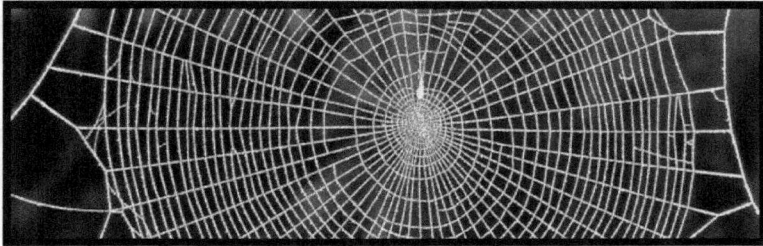

An example of a complex web of an orb weaver, a type of spider that constructs a web to catch its prey. Some spiders do not construct webs and catch their prey by searching the ground or plants.

"Well," said Jason, "you certainly have given me a scare, but I can see that what you do is necessary. How do you catch the insects when they fly into your web though, Mr. Spider?"

"Let's get one thing straight. I'm Mrs. Spider. Mr. Spider is that little guy at the edge of my web. He's a lot smaller than I am.

An insect that had gotten caught in a spider's web. Once caught, the spider typically moves to the insect and goes about shooting out silk and wrapping the insect in it. It may be fed upon or saved for later.

"To answer your question, my web is a little sticky, as you have found out, so when an insect flies into it, it sticks on the web until I can get there."

"But how do you know you've caught something?" Jason asked.

"Well, when they hit the web and try to escape, it jiggles and lets me know something got caught. When I rush over to get it, I shoot out some special silk from the tip of my abdomen and wrap the insect in it. Then when I'm hungry, I bite my prey, inject some saliva into it and suck out my food."

"What do you mean you suck out your food?"

"I don't have mouthparts to chew with, so what I have to do is inject some saliva into the insects so it can digest their tissue. Then I suck the juice up, something like you humans drink a milk shake."

Jason said, "That sounds disgusting."

"Maybe it does, but that's how we spiders have to do it. We don't have much choice about how we eat. Basically, we digest our food before we eat it, whereas you humans and most other animals digest food after you eat it. In a way, though, it's the same process."

"I suppose so." He still had a disgusted look on his face. Whether it was the same process or not, Jason didn't think he could eat his food in that way. "What else do you do here?"

Female spider with a large number of spiderlings on her back. Not all spiders do this, but it is relatively common in certain types of spiders.

"I sometimes mate, and then I build an egg case of silk, into which I deposit my eggs. I leave my egg case attached to my web, but some of my relatives carry their egg cases around with them. When the eggs hatch, my young spiders, spiderlings as you humans call them, come out and begin to catch things on their own.

"I don't ever take care of them like some animals do. The young of some spiders stay with their mother for a while after they hatch, but mine just go off and have to fend for themselves. Sometimes, they stay around my web, but as they grow up, they begin to build their own web."

Jason asked, "Well, if there are so many young spiders around, where are they?"

"Young spiderlings use different methods to go from where they hatch to a new location. Some do crawl off or crawl up trees and hang from a strand of silk until they reach a new area, but there are many more fascinating methods of getting around."

This puzzled Jason, and he asked, "What do you mean?"

"As you walk through the field on a warm summer day, you should watch closely. Many young spiders crawl to the tops of plants and release a strand of silk that floats up into the wind.

"When the strand gets long enough, the wind catches it and picks the spiderling up, kind of like parasailing, and it floats to a new destination by wind currents. You humans call this process ballooning.

"Spiderlings that do this don't have control over where they are going because it's up to the wind to carry them to different places, but it is known that they can be carried to great heights and over great distances. When they finally land, they construct a web and begin catching their own insects.

"My life is a little easier than some of my orb-weaving relatives. Some of them remove and build their webs almost every day. That's an awful lot of work. I just keep mine as long as I can, and I repair it when it gets holes in it.

Jason said, "It appears that I destroyed several parts of your web when I ran into it. I apologize. I didn't even see it when I was walking."

"Oh, don't worry about it. Other animals run into it all the time. That's the beauty of a web. Insects don't see it either, and that's how they get caught.

"I'll just crawl around and check out the damage and begin repairing it after you leave. I have to be ready for any insects that fly through, you know. That's a price I have to pay for building such an elaborate web."

Jason once again appeared confused and asked, "Do all spiders build webs as fancy as yours?"

Spiders make their egg cases (left) from silk that is produced by their bodies and spun from abdominal structures called spinnerets (right). They also use their silk to wrap their prey until they can be eaten. Many types of insects also make silk, but it is often produced in glands in their heads.

"Oh no," the spider said. "Some of my spider relatives don't even build webs at all. They just walk around and look for their food, and when they find it, they jump on it. Some of these types are wolf spiders, water spiders and tarantulas. One of my relatives, the jumping spider, can see very well and sometimes jumps long distances on flies before they even have a chance to fly away.

"There are other spiders that build a web, but it may be funnel-shaped, a small, flat web or have no particular arrangement whatsoever. Go into a field early in the morning on a summer day, and you'll see thousands of small webs that stand out because of the dew that collects on them. It almost looks like jewels in the sun. It's really a pretty sight.

"Let's get back to your question about the types of webs we build. It just depends on the type of spider that's making it."

"I know what you mean," Jason said. "I saw some of the spiders you are talking about with funnel-shaped webs in the area with all the logs. I also saw one come out and grab an insect. I couldn't talk to it, though, because it ran right back through its funnel before I had a chance to say anything."

"It's good you had a chance to see that," said the spider. "Most people don't take the time to watch things like that. You'll find that the webs of spiders and the ways they use them vary tremendously.

"Take the tarantulas, for instance. Most of them are quite large, and they live in holes in the ground or in some protected area. They spin a little silk, but the arrangement of the silk is poorly defined. They hunt at night by walking around. Much of my catching of insects is during the day or during the twilight hours, and I prefer to have my food come to me.

"There are some spiders that you humans call trap door spiders that live in holes, and they build a little door over the hole. When something edible comes along, they throw their door open and rapidly pounce upon their prey. Some of those spiders have a poison that can seriously harm humans if they are bitten.

"The widow spiders, like the black widow, red widow and brown widow, all make poorly defined webs, and they usually put them in places that are hidden from view, like under benches, tables, chairs, and logs. You should be very careful putting your hands beneath things in areas where the widow spiders are found."

Black widow spider, one of the spiders with an especially potent venom. It is shown here with a poorly formed web. There are brown widow spiders that are not quite as colorful as this type.

"I guess that's why my cousin, David, taught me to use a potato rake to roll things with. I thank you for telling me more about this, Mrs. Spider. I will be careful.

"Let me ask you one final question before I leave. I've heard that some spiders, like the widows you mentioned, are dangerous for humans. Why is that?"

"Well, there are many types of venoms produced by spiders. Some are more dangerous than others. For some reason, the widows have a very potent venom. There are many of their close relatives that have the same body size and shape but are not nearly as dangerous.

"You'll notice that some of the most dangerous ones have markings on their body that are easy for someone to recognize. Take the black widow, for instance. The female has a bright red hour glass-like marking on the bottom of her black abdomen. By knowing these patterns and bright, contrasting colors, animals learn to stay away from them."

Jason said, "The mantid told me about these things in insects. Are all the dangerous spiders like that, with bright colors and obvious patterns?"

"Unfortunately, they're not. There are some very dangerous ones that have common colors and patterns. Take the brown recluse spider, for instance. It's a brown color just like many other spiders, but it's very dangerous. Its venom usually isn't deadly, but it causes a bitten animal's skin and flesh to die, and the wound becomes a serious problem."

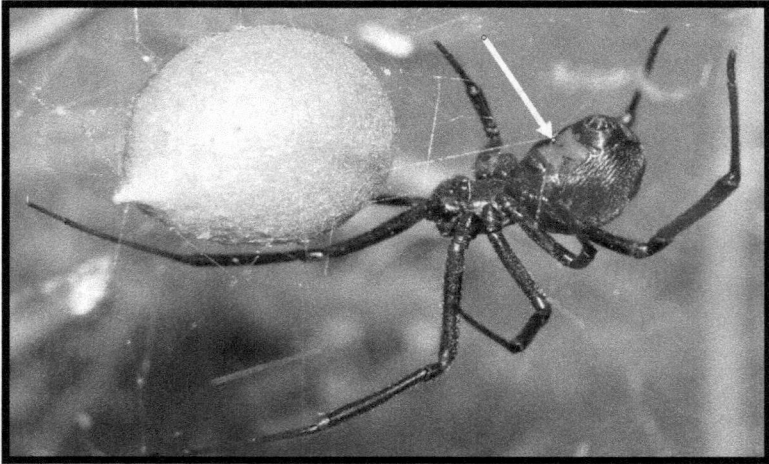

Black widow female with an egg case. Bright, contrasting colors on spiders (arrow pointing to a red hour-glass shape on the abdomen) and insects generally mean that they are dangerous in some way, although many organisms support bright, contrasting patterns because they mimic the dangerous types, even though they may not be dangerous.

"I hope I never run into one of those. I appreciate all you've told me. You are very interesting. Is there anything you'd like to add to what you've told me?"

Before the spider had a chance to think and say a word, Jason came up with a new question. "I would imagine most animals are afraid of spiders like you. Is that true?" Jason remarked.

"Well, many animals may be afraid, but there are a lot of animals that can eat us too. Birds often look for us, and so do lizards and many insects. There are even wasps that specialize in catching spiders."

"Wow, it's not safe for anyone out here. I hope you do well. I hate to leave you here, but I must move to another spot in the environment," Jason said. "I hope you catch a lot of things in your web so you can have more offspring." As he moved away, the spider immediately began checking her net to make repairs.

⑬

The King Snake

Since Jason had just barely entered the woodland habitat, he remained in the vicinity of the woodland edge and noticed another log he felt he could move. He thought he had been finished with rolling them, but this one looked especially intriguing. It was a little larger than the others, and it was positioned on top of a smaller log so there was some space beneath it for something larger than insects to hide in.

With his potato rake, he pulled repeatedly at various parts of it until it finally became dislodged from the ground and began to move. With one powerful yank, he rolled it and discovered a black and white snake beneath it that was as long as his arm. As he stared at the snake, observing its beautiful pattern and sleek, shiny body, it began to move slightly.

Not wanting to lose the opportunity to talk with him like he had done with the insects and spiders that had run away before he could get their attention, he said, "Wait, please don't go. I would like to talk with you. I'm so sorry I disturbed you, but I couldn't help rolling this log to see what was underneath it."

"Well you found out, alright. But it's OK, as long as you don't want to hurt me.. What do you want to know?"

Who are you, anyway?"

The snake suddenly came to a halt, grew in size and looked up at Jason, finally answering, "I'm a king snake. I was resting here after having a good meal."

"I am really sorry I turned your log over and disturbed you. I'll turn it back over when I leave, and you can go back to getting your rest, but before I leave, could you please tell me what you do here?"

"As you may have guessed, I like to hide most of the time. Many of the other snakes spend more time out in the open. I do get out in the sun occasionally, and when I'm out, I'm usually looking for some type of food.

"What is it that you eat, king snake?"

"I eat mice, lizards and occasional birds and other snakes. Once in a while, I eat eggs. I only eat when the weather is warm though. When the winter comes, I usually hibernate in a log or down in a hole somewhere."

"Well," Jason said, "why do you sun yourself? Are you trying to get a sun tan?"

The king snake laughed a little, followed it with a little hissing sound, and said, "No, of course not. I have a problem that you humans don't have. I heard that you talked to a blue racer and he talked about it already, but I'll repeat it for you. I can't produce body heat as well as you and many other types of animals can, so I lie out in the sun for a little while and absorb the heat before I can become very active. If it's a little cool, I can't move very fast, and my body doesn't function very well until I get warm. Of course, if I stay out in the sun too long, I can get too hot.

"Now I remember what he said, Jason commented. Are you and the blue racer the only animals that have to rely on the sun to get warm?"

"Oh, no. There are many others. All snakes, lizards, turtles, alligators, crocodiles, frogs, salamanders, insects and insect-like creatures depend on the sun to get warm. When it gets very cold, that's when we have to hibernate."

"What is hibernation, anyway?"

"It's a kind of condition animals experience when it is cold. The animals that can't control their temperature very well find a safe place to stay during the winter months, and they go into a kind of sleep until the weather warms up. For me, a hole or under a log, or even inside a log is usually a safe place to be during winter. In colder climates, many snakes have to go deeper into the ground. Some places on earth, like Alaska, get too cold during the winter, so many things like snakes can't even live there.

"Things that live in the water, like fish, alligators, crocodiles, frogs and salamanders, can somehow go deeper in the water so they can avoid the very cold weather. However, most of them have to get into the sun to get warmer, too, when they finally do come out of hibernation.

"In the spring of the year, when the weather finally becomes a little warm, we come out of hibernation and have to warm up in the sun before we can eat. Once we're warm, though, we can sometimes move very fast."

Jason said, "I've heard that you won't die if a poisonous snake bites you. Is that true?"

"Why yes, it is. We don't like to be bitten though, but for some reason, we king snakes are immune to those venoms. It's a good thing because I run into one once in a while."

"If you see the blue racer, don't eat him. He's my friend."

"Oh yes, I've seen him on occasion. He's very fast. Tell him to be careful."

Jason asked, "What about having young snakes? I would imagine you have those during the warm months."

"Yes, that's true. It's usually in the spring that we find a mate and have our young ones. Many snakes, including me and the blue racer, lay eggs, while others have live young. Some of the egg-layers besides us are rat snakes, hog nosed snakes, and many of the smaller types. Some snake types that have live young are water snakes, ribbon snakes, garter snakes, and most of the poisonous snakes in North America.

"Of course, the young snakes that are born just wiggle out of their membranes and can crawl right off, but the young in eggs have to develop before they can hatch. We have to be careful where we lay our eggs because other things can eat them."

"What do you mean?"

"Well, when we are ready to lay our eggs, we try to find a hidden spot, like under or in a log. That way, they are more difficult to find. I'm sure the blue racer told you this. Our eggs have soft shells, unlike those of a bird, and they have to remain in a damp environment or they will shrivel up and die. All their development goes on in the egg.

Jason commented, "Yes, the blue racer said the same thing, but I don't remember how the little snakes get out of the egg?"

In order for young snakes to get out of their eggs, they slit the egg with a hard structure on the tip of their nose. Once they emerge, the egg tooth is lost.

"When their development is complete," said the king snake, "they have a hard little tooth-like device on their noses, called an egg tooth by you humans, and they use it to slice holes in the egg so they can get out. They poke their little heads out and look around and eventually leave the egg.

"Sometimes, their body patterns when they first hatch are much different from what they will be when they become an adult. Take that blue racer you talked about as an example. When the young first hatch out of the egg, they have a pattern of blotches all over them. They're really cute. As they get older, they lose the blotches and end up one solid color. Some people say that the blotched pattern helps the young snakes hide in their environment. Some snakes, like many rat snakes, never lose their blotches."

Jason said, "The blue racer told me that he walked on his ribs. Do you do that too?"

"Why, yes, I do, but some snakes walk on their ribs more than others. Sometimes we also wiggle our bodies so we can use the plants or the ground we're walking over to move more rapidly.

Snake skeleton, showing numerous ribs which move back and forth along the ground to move the snake forward. Snakes also move their body from side to side to push themselves onward.

"Some of us snakes are relatively slow when we move, and others are very fast. I don't usually go very fast, but if something is chasing me, I can move along at a pretty rapid pace. I'm never as fast as the blue racer though.

"You'll find that different snakes react in different ways to the presence of humans or other animals. Some just lie still, hoping that they can stay hidden. Some try to crawl to a hidden spot. Some stay in one place and raise their heads so they can bite whoever it is that's disturbing them. Even the poisonous types will try to get away sometimes."

Jason said, "But why would they run away? People are usually afraid of them."

"That's true. Many humans are afraid of snakes, but most of us can't harm them. Also, snakes are afraid of humans too. Some humans will kill any of us. They don't seem to understand that we are living, breathing creatures like everyone else, and we often do a lot of good for our community."

"What do you mean when you say you do a lot of good?" Jason asked.

"We are like many predators out in our habitats. We feed on many rodents that can eat crops or become pests in your homes. Can you imagine how big the rodent population would get if there weren't predators like us to eat some of them? We help in the balance of nature.

"There are many animals that you could look at and wonder what their role is in the balance of nature. For example, take the raccoon, the possum, the fox, or many of the animals that you may run across out in nature. When you first think about their place in nature, you may have trouble understanding what they do that is good for their particular habitat. Yet, each one has a certain role to play, and eliminating any one of them may cause shifts in the population of other animals in that particular habitat.

"I hate to say it, but I could ask the same question about you humans. What good are you for the different habitats we all live in? In many ways, it's been the humans who have destroyed more habitats than any other animal on earth. So when you think about it, who's the most dangerous animal on our planet?"

"I hate to admit it," said Jason, "but we humans are pretty irresponsible when it comes to the environment, but I think the grown-ups are trying to do better. I think they're trying to preserve areas and keep the environment in mind when they want to use the land."

"Well," said the king snake, "I just hope your population doesn't get so large that you use all the land for your living and building space. If you do, I believe the other living things in the world are going to suffer from it."

"Maybe I can talk to people and tell them what I'm learning," Jason said, "and it will help them understand the plight we're all in. Thanks for talking to me. What you told me is something I have to think about a lot. I hope to see you again."

With his last words, Jason said goodbye to the king snake, rolled the log back into place, and moved deeper into the woods, all the while thinking about what the king snake had told him. He began to worry more about his future and the future of all the other wild animals out in nature.

⑭

The Deer

A s Jason got deeper into the woods, he once again felt the chill and dampness of a habitat that could harbor many types of animals of various sizes and types that he had not seen in other habitats. As on the earlier trip with David, there were no harsh breezes to desiccate the woodland's small creatures, and it was a place that could readily be used by larger animals, as well.

In some ways, it was both gloomy and peaceful, unlike any of the other habitats he had experienced. He couldn't explain it, but he felt farther away from civilization here than he had felt since the time he had entered the strange and enchanted land he was now experiencing.

As he enjoyed the quiet, he stooped down and looked along the forest floor to find creatures of small size. He then raised himself to a more erect position and was suddenly looking directly into the eyes of a deer. Without hearing a sound made by its approach, it was as though it just appeared from nowhere.

It didn't have antlers, so he presumed it was a doe. Initially, he was speechless and studied the animal's kind but attentive eyes. It was as if he was looking into the depth of cautiousness.

In spite of the deer's vigilance, it somehow knew Jason wasn't a threat. Yet, it didn't move a muscle, and they both stared at one another for what felt like an eternity.

Finally, in a soft voice so as not to break the peace, Jason said, "Are you a deer?"

"Why, yes, I am," said the deer, "and not just any deer. I'm a white tailed deer. I'm also a doe, like the song, 'doe, a deer, a female deer.' And what about you?"

"I'm a boy, and I'm trying to learn about the animals out here in nature. Could you please tell me what you are doing here in the woods?"

The tail of a whitetail deer flashes behind it as it runs through the forest. There are many species of deer around the world.

The deer said, "Of course. It will be my pleasure. I live here. Sometimes I run into the fields, but that's usually early in the morning, late in the evening, or at night time. I have to be very careful when I leave the woods. It's sometimes dangerous for me to go into the fields during the day."

Jason asked, "Why are those times so dangerous?"

"It's mostly because of you humans. You see, I have to be careful to avoid hunters. I'm too easy to see during the day time, so when most of the people go to bed, I come out and begin to search for food and enjoy my other activities."

"But it's not hunting season. Aren't you safe now?"

"Not really. In the first place, I don't know when this hunting season you speak of starts and stops except that's when I see a lot of people with guns out here in the woods. That's when I'm most cautious.

"There are some people, though, that don't care if it's hunting season or not. If they see a deer, they shoot it. They don't care that we're living, breathing animals just like they are. Some of them just want to shoot us for the pleasure of killing something."

"That's terrible," said Jason. "I don't understand why someone would do something like that. I really can't comprehend why people want to kill deer even during hunting season."

"Well," said the deer, "in many ways, humans are still very primitive animals. They have progressed in their technology to levels that are amazing, but many of them still have retained this desire to kill. Then, there are other reasons that they have come up with to kill members of our populations."

"What reasons are those?" asked Jason.

"In a way, I can understand why humans feel they have to cull our populations on occasion. You keep using new places in nature to build your houses, other buildings, roads and farms, and this puts our populations in a stressful position.

"It's not just your fault. We deer are just like any other animal in that we try to produce more offspring than our habitat can handle. Sometimes, our populations get to be very large, over-populous as you humans call it.

"When this happens in nature, the populations generally begin to suffer from diseases, this being the way that nature weeds out the weaker animals. When we have too many of us in a population, many of the weaker individuals die, and this stabilizes our population once again.

"There are other things that happen when groups of animals become overpopulated, but most of it falls under the heading of stress."

Jason asked, "What do you mean by stress?"

"There are all kinds of stresses that enter the lives of animals in nature. They are usually in the form of competition for food, dominance, a mate, and the territory that we occupy. You see, we attempt to be dominant so we can have our choice of a place to live and all the food we want. This also allows us to have some clout when we choose our mate. In addition, it determines how much space we each will have around us. We animals all need our space.

"You may be surprised that I say this, but you humans have population problems too. It makes no difference if it's a cage of mice or a population of humans. When populations grow too large, there are problems of all sorts that emerge. Just look at what's happening in your populations right now.

"Of course, your wars are your business. We other animals have not developed the sophisticated methods of culling a population as you have.

"Personally, I feel we all should let our natural populations take care of themselves, but you humans seem to think that you need to stabilize our populations through hunting. Believe me, that's a human approach to our problems.

"This is why I may get shot. I don't mean any harm to anyone. I just want to walk around, browse on plants, and be left alone."

Jason said, "Well, you've given me a lot to think about. I'm not sure we humans always understand the ways of nature. You're right. We have gotten ourselves in a lot of trouble, but let's get back to you. You said you browse. What exactly does that mean?"

"I feed on plants, so I'm called an herbivore, but there are different ways of feeding. You're probably familiar with the way horses and cows eat. They mostly graze on grasses and plants on the ground. We deer browse, which means we feed on plants like bushes and shrubs.

"That's primarily what I eat. Most of the plants I eat are here in the woodland or at the edge, next to the open field. Of course, I may do a little grazing once in a while as well."

Jason said, "You're a very big animal. Are there any animals in nature that can hurt you?

"Not here," the deer said, "but there are some places that cougars, dogs, coyotes, and wolves can catch us. The puma population here has been dwindling over the years, so they really haven't been a problem for us. Fortunately for us, there are very few predators in these parts, except for an occasional bob cat. Even if there were, we most often can protect ourselves from predators."

Jason asked, "How do you do that?"

"Our adults are always looking for danger, and when we see it, we can run to safety very quickly. We also hide very well in our habitat. Our young even have spots to help them blend into the environment. This is especially important because if a predator finds our young, there's not much they can do to defend themselves. Another protective feature in our young is the absence of a scent. A predator can sometimes be right next to one of them and still not know they're there. Humans call our young fawns."

"When do you have your young?"

"We usually have them in the summer or early fall of the year, when the food is most plentiful. We generally have one young at a time, similar to you humans.

A young deer with spots. Spots help them blend in with their environment. As they get older, they lose their spots.

"We treat our young like you humans treat yours in some ways. We feed them milk that we make in our bodies when they're very young, and we try to teach them how to live in our environment. By living, I mostly mean learning what to eat and how to be careful."

"Yes, that's very important for any animal. Well, I must move on, so

good luck, and thanks for talking to me."
    "It's my pleasure," said the deer.

⑮

The Possum

As Jason moved even deeper into the woodland habitat where the trees were taller and formed a thicker canopy over the smaller vegetation, the next animal he saw was a possum, who for some reason, was clearly showing signs of being afraid. He hunched his back, showed his teeth and hissed at Jason.

Knowing the true nature of this animal because of what David had told him earlier, Jason said, "Oh, cut your act. I'm not going to hurt you. I just want to talk to you. I've already talked to many of your friends, so please calm down and tell me what you're doing here."

Since Jason didn't actually appear to be a threat to him, the possum immediately quit his pretending and said, "I'm sorry for my bad temper."

Jason said, "Oh, that's alright. I can understand your concern. I'd probably do the same thing if someone startled me. Tell me a little about yourself."

"I am an opossum, possum for short. I usually stay in holes or under vegetation during the day, and most of my activity is at night.

"You just caught me at an odd moment, and I didn't see you coming. That's why I reacted the way I did. When I'm alone and out of my more pro-tected places, I generally roam around, looking for food.

Jason said, "What kinds of foods do you eat, possum?"

"I eat just about anything, like berries, different plants, and some-times even meat from animals that have died."

Jason said, "That doesn't seem very appealing. Why do you eat those things?"

"Well, that's just what we eat. You'll find that out here in nature, there are animals that eat just about anything. I don't know why. I just do it."

Not quite satisfied with the answer he got, Jason decided to change the subject and said, "I've heard that you play dead sometimes. Why do you do that?"

"It's interesting that you ask that question. Acting like that isn't really something we can control. When it appears that something or someone is going to harm us, we sometimes go into this behavior that almost puts us in a trance. We fall over and look dead. What else can I say? It sometimes looks ridiculous, but sometimes it protects us from having a confrontation with another animal. If we confront them, we may get hurt in the process.

"Actually, you may be surprised to know that there are many animals that do this. Your scientists call it death-feigning. Hog-nose snakes are fa-mous for their death-feigning behavior. They even roll over on their back and hang their tongue out. Also, there are many insects that do it, so, you see, it's a behavior that is relatively common in the animal kingdom.

"You're probably aware of this, but animals do all sorts of things when they are in a threatening situation. Death-feigning is just one of our reactions to defend ourselves."

"What other things do you do?"

"You've seen some of what I do. I show my teeth and hiss. This makes me appear meaner than I really am, but I do it to scare someone that I think is going to hurt me. I also hump my back, trying to make my body look bigger than it really is, and then I sometimes make the hair stand up on my body for the same reason.

A skunk, with bright, contrasting colors, is said to have a warning coloration. When it is threatened, it raises its tail and back and sprays a most-unpleasant fluid from its anal area as a means of protecting itself from harm.

"Some animals have colorations or patterns to help them blend in with other things in their environment. It's a form of mimicry, and it's another way for an animal to defend itself."

Jason said, "Oh, yes, the mantid told me about that in different insects, and he also said that if I ever talked to you I should ask you about the different ways other animals defend themselves. Can you give me some other examples?"

"Sure. Many animals have young that have spots or blotches on their bodies that help them blend in with the vegetation in their environment. I think the deer would tell you about this when talking about its fawns. Stripes function in the same way. Zebras are very good examples of that. While this is interesting in itself, there are many more extraordinary examples of this in nature.

"There are butterflies, like the Indian Leaf Butterfly, that look like a leaf when it folds its wings. The leaves that it resembles are on a plant upon which the butterfly lands. It's pretty amazing.

Indian leaf butterfly. Although the upper side of their wings are brightly colored, the underside (as seen here) is drab, appearing like a dead leaf. This is a cryptic type of mimicry in which the butterfly's appearance helps it blend in with other parts of its environment, which hides it from potential predators.

"Many mantids and walking sticks, as you know, are colored like the vegetation in their habitat, and they sometimes have body structures that look like the vegetation. You could be looking directly at one and not see it.

"There are many other examples of this in nature. We could talk about them all day, but other forms of defense by animals are sometimes even more amazing, although they are usually more difficult to understand. Take alarm patterns and colors, for instance."

Jason remarked, "Oh, yes. That was another topic that was covered by the mantid. Certain patterns and bright colors make some animals stand out, and they usually have other qualities that help protect them, like poisonous or unpleasant chemicals in their body. I would like to hear about other examples."

"I'm impressed with what you have learned out here," the possum said, "Have you ever seen a skunk?"

"No, I haven't," said Jason, "but my cousin, David, told me about them. Would you tell me what you know about them?"

"Sure. Skunks are animals that have the contrasting colors of black and white in their fur. When you see one, there is no question about what it is. They can produce extremely foul-smelling chemicals from special glands in their body when they are afraid, and they can spray them on you. Most people that have alarmed a skunk will never forget the experience. They also sometimes hump their back and raise their tail as a warning.

"The monarch butterfly is another example. If a bird sees a monarch butterfly caterpillar and it tries to eat it, it will spit it out, and it may even get sick because the caterpillar has foul tasting chemicals it got from the plants that it eats. The caterpillar is easy to see by all animals because it has black, white, and yellow markings on its body. The adult butterflies also taste bad and have bright colors.

"The bright colors and contrasting pattern help to make both the caterpillar and adult stand out in its environment, but it also helps birds remember not to eat one of them. If a bird sees another such caterpillar or adult, it will most certainly leave either of them alone."

Jason said, "You've given me an example of this in one butterfly, but is this that common in nature?"

"Oh, yes. There are thousands of examples. It's fairly common in butterflies, especially tropical ones, and in many other insects, and it's not only distasteful or bad smelling chemicals that are involved. Some insects bite, some have stinging hairs on their body and others have a sting at the end of their body.

"Most animals that have these types of defenses usually warn someone who is approaching them before they use their defensive tactics. Even the skunk will sometimes try to warn someone before it sprays chemicals on them. Of course, if the animal feels it is in immediate danger, it may skip the warnings and rapidly go into a more direct approach to defending itself.

"Wasps that make a paper nest are other examples of this. They usually have markings on their body with black, brown, or orange, and they demonstrate many behaviors that are easy for all of us to see and remember.

"When someone approaches their nest, they usually demonstrate behaviors like quick body movements, leg waving, wing raising and wing waving before they come off the nest to sting. These things generally warn another animal to stay away.

"Of course, if they persist in going toward the nest, they will get stung."

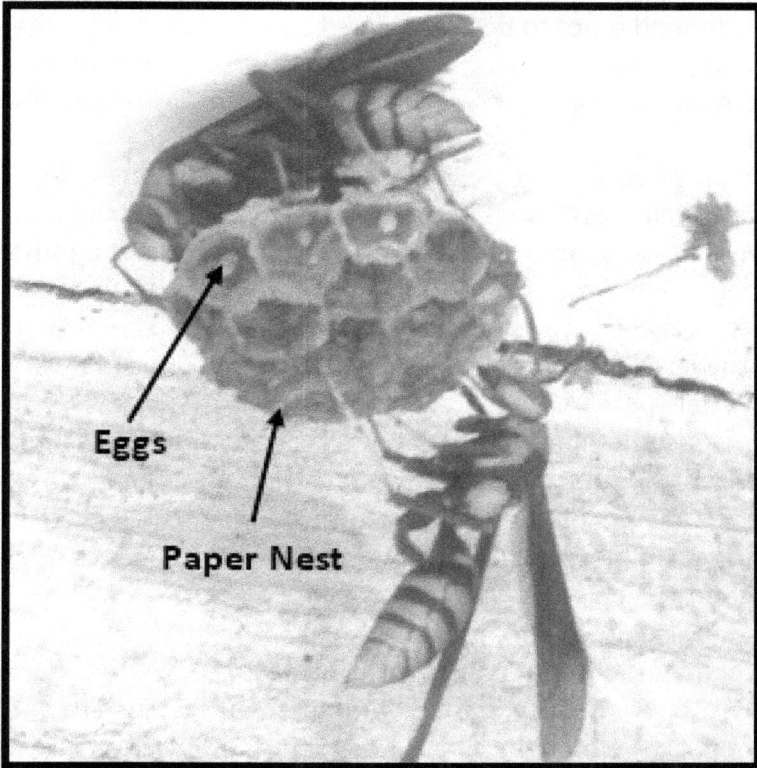

A paper wasp and its colony. These wasps make their nest by scraping wood with their mouthparts and making a paper mache type material. When it gets back to its nest, it lays the paper mache down to form cells, in which they raise their young. Since they have a colony, they are very defensive if the colony is threatened.

Jason said, "I can understand how this warning system works. If you're one of these animals, and something approaches your nest, you would rather warn them then get into a fight. Warning is an attempt to scare them so they'll go away. If you fight, you could lose, maybe even lose your life. If you warn them, and they go away, you don't have to fight. It's a way of avoiding a fight. The mantid also said something about this."

"You've learned your lesson well, Jason," said the possum. "Some animals don't warn you in a very clear manner though. Fire ants are a good example of that. If you step on one of their mounds, the workers rush out and sting you immediately. There is no apparent warning, but in other, more subtle ways, they do warn you. Once you've stepped on such a mound, you learn that a mound is not to be approached. The mound itself is the warning signal. It's not a bright color or contrasting colors, but it's something that stands out in the environment, and we all learn what will happen if we tangle with them."

"This is all very interesting," said Jason. "I never would have guessed that animals do all these things until the mantid mentioned them to me. And you've given me so many good examples. I suppose this is another reason why we should look closer at things in nature."

"Yes, it is," said the possum. "If you live out in nature long enough, you learn to watch for things like this. Otherwise, you may be very uncomfortable out here.

"Here's something to think about," said the possum. Humans warn each other, do they not? What happens when one human threatens another? What behavior do they demonstrate?"

"Wow. This is a lot to think about. I'll have to get back to you on that."

"I hope you do," said the possum."

"What else do you do, possum?"

"We mate sometimes and have babies, but we're different from most of the other animals in our environment. Our babies are born before they finish their development. At the time of birth, they crawl to a pouch we have on our bellies, and they stay in that pouch until they have completed their development.

"In this respect, we're something like kangaroos, wallabies, and other animals in Australia. Humans call animals like us marsupials, and we opossums are the only marsupials that live in nature in America.

"Humans consider us very primitive as mammals. One reason they think this is because we have a very small and poorly developed brain."

Jason asked, "Hold on a minute, possum. What is a mammal? I remember talking about it with one of the animals I've spoken to, but I can't remember what they said."

"A mammal is an animal that has hair on its body and produces milk. Most of the large animals you know are mammals, like dogs, cats, cows, pigs, horses, monkeys, rhinos, hippos, lions, and tigers. Humans are mammals too."

Jason asked, "So, you possums are considered primitive mammals. Is there any mammals more primitive than you?"

"In terms of how we have our young, there actually are animals that are more primitive than us, but they're not in the United States. They are called monotremes, examples being two Australian animals called the echidna and platypus. They're the only mammals in the world that lay eggs.

"To finish answering your earlier question, when our young get older, we go on short trips so we can teach them to survive in the environment. Most animals that are endotherms do this. Sometimes we even hang by our tails."

"There you go again, possum, using terms I'm not completely familiar with. What do you mean by endotherms?"

"Well, animals like mammals and birds, produce enough heat in their bodies to keep them at a certain temperature. We don't have to lay in the sun to be warm like the reptiles do. That's why some people call them cold blooded, although that's not quite accurate. Their blood can be warm if they are out in the sun long enough or in a warm climate. They just can't produce body heat like we can. Actually, I believe your scientists more correctly call animals that can't produce their own body heat ectotherms because they get their body heat from outside sources. Ecto means outside, and endo means inside."

"That's very interesting," Jason said. "I remember now that the blue racer told me about how he has to lay out in the sun to get warm. There are so many different types of animals and also ways that they must learn to live in their environment, and they all seem to fit into nature. I'm sure you fit in too."

"Yes, we have a place in nature. As you know, we're all part of the food chain and balance in the natural world. There are animals, like bob cats, foxes, and wolves that try to eat us, and we help clean up the natural environment of things by eating some of them. We may not be a major contributor to our habitat, but we have our part."

"I would think that what you do is very important. Are there any other things that I should know about you?"

"Well, there is one thing. I hate to mention it because it's difficult to deal with, but my two strongest fears have to do with humans."

Jason asked, "How's that, possum?"

"I'm afraid that humans are taking much of our woodland, and when this happens, we have to move our homes. Sometimes we get killed because of your progress, and when we move, we sometimes go out on the roads. I would guess that most of us lose our lives on your roads. It's not only us that are having trouble with this. Most wild animals have problems understanding that roads are dangerous places for us to go."

"I'll try to tell people to be careful when they're out on the road so they don't hit you."

"Thanks," said the possum. "I'd appreciate that."

"I've taken up enough of your time," Jason said. "Thanks for all the information. You've helped me to understand your world much better. Enjoy yourself, and be careful."

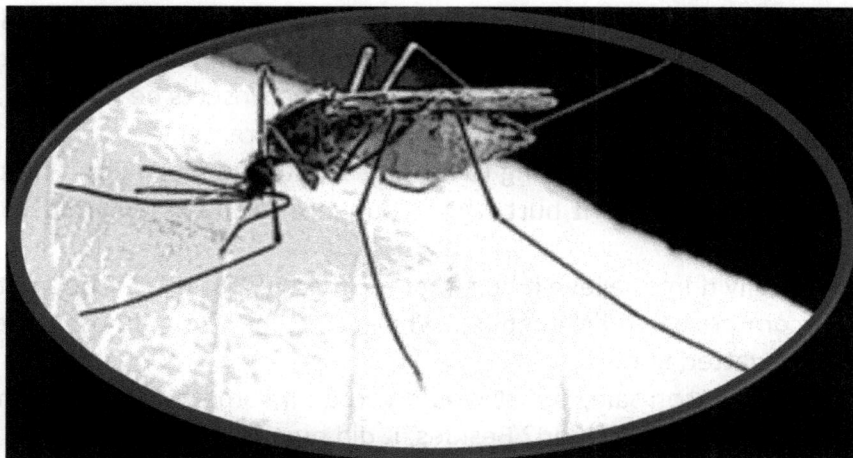

⑯

The Mosquito

As Jason inched his way down a hill toward the lake, he once again passed through the wet area that he and David had walked through earlier. He visualized the leeches that latched onto his ankles and hoped he wouldn't have to share his blood with them on this trip.

Hearing the humming sounds of insects flying around him was a little annoying, but they seemed to be different from those of the flies he had experienced earlier. Suddenly, he felt a slight stinging feeling on the back of his right arm, and he reeled around to slap whatever it was with his left hand. When he did this, a mosquito narrowly escaped the swat and flew up to land on a nearby leaf.

As Jason stared at the insect, he realized its fat belly was sporting a dark reddish coloration from the blood he had taken from him. He briefly took his attention off the mosquito to survey the area for more of the blood-suckers, and when he turned back around, the little mosquito that had fed on him had suddenly become as large as the other insects he had seen, and its long hypodermic-like beak was now huge and threatening.

"That wasn't a nice thing to do," he said to the mosquito. "That was my blood you took, and it hurt when you were taking it. Why did you do that?"

"I really don't believe it hurt that much, boy, but there's bound to be some discomfort when I'm feeding. What about me? You almost killed me when you swatted at me."

"Well," Jason said, "what would you do if something landed on you and began to suck your blood? Besides, it did hurt."

"I apologize, but as a mosquito, I have to inject some chemicals that will keep your blood from clotting while I'm feeding so it will keep flowing through my long, thin mouthparts. That's what causes the stinging feeling you get. I don't really try to hurt you. It would be better for me if I got my blood and flew away without you even knowing it."

"Well, mosquito, it's a very unpleasant feeling, to say the least. Do you have to take blood from people?"

"It's not just people that I take blood from. I take it from whatever animal is out here in my habitat, and yes, it is necessary for me to take blood. I can't live without it. Just as you have to eat to stay alive, I have to suck blood, and blood is also necessary for me to lay eggs.

"What I do is this. Once I get my blood, I look for a place to lay my eggs. It's usually at a spot just above the water line in a moist environment. Some other mosquitoes lay their eggs on the water or even make little boats to float their eggs on.

"My eggs stay where I put them until a rain comes, and when the water level goes up and covers them, they hatch, and a larval stage is re-leased from each egg into the water to live there until it develops further. It has no legs to move around with, so it wiggles around through the water. Because of this behavior, you humans call this stage in my life cycle a wiggler stage. The wiggler breathes in its aquatic environment through a hole on its rear end.

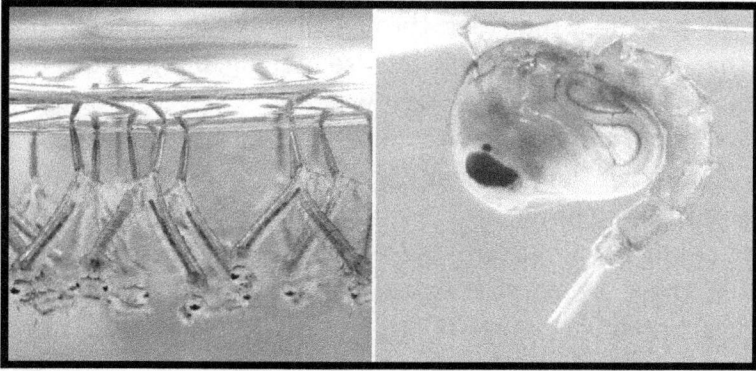

Left, mosquito larvae putting their breathing tubes through the surface of the water to breath. Right, a mosquito pupa with its back to the water surface so that it can breathe.

"It goes through a number of periods where it sheds its skin and becomes larger. Once it reaches its maximum size, it undergoes its last molt and becomes a pupa. Since the pupa's movement in the water is accomplished by a tumbling motion, humans refer to this stage in our life cycle as a tumbler stage. It breathes by putting its back at the water surface. This is the stage in which we change from our larval form to become an adult like me.

"An adult mosquito emerges through a slit in the pupa's back and flies off to harden before it seeks a blood meal. After it feeds on some animal, it develops eggs and repeats the entire process. That's how our life goes, over and over again."

"But why blood?" Jason couldn't understand the significance of feeding in this way.

"It's just another way to feed, and that's just about all our beaks can function to do. Of course, we are known to feed on nectar at times. Our males can't suck blood, so the only nourishment they get is by feeding on nectar. It's only us females that can suck blood, and we are among the many different animals that are called blood-feeding parasites. It's our way of life."

Jason said, "You mean there are other things that feed like you do?"

"Oh, yes. There are many. I think you ran into at least one of them on your last trip through here. You do remember the leeches, don't you?"

"Yes, I certainly do," said Jason, "but I don't remember feeling it when they were feeding."

"Some parasites that feed through the skin of animals inject some chemicals that numb the skin while they're feeding, but it doesn't always kill all the pain. All we can do is try as best we can."

"What other things suck blood? I'll have to watch out for them."

"There are a lot of flies that suck blood. I'm one of them. I'll bet you didn't know I'm a type of fly."

"No, I didn't." said Jason.

"Then, there are horse flies, deer flies, black flies, and no-see-ums. I believe you also had deer flies flying around your head on your last trip through here. Do you remember that?"

"Oh, yes," said Jason. "They were very annoying, now that I think about it."

"What's interesting is that the mouthparts of many of these flies are different from mine, even though they feed on blood. Many of them have blades that cut the skin, and when blood flows out, they lap it up. Some flies cause bleeding by scraping the skin with their mouthparts. The feeding by most of these flies hurts more than when I get my blood meal."

Jason asked, "How do you know all this?"

"I'm a parasite, so I know a little about our way of life, but humans have studied the different ways of feeding. It's all in books. All you have to do is find the right books."

"You mentioned flies called no-see-ums. That's a pretty strange name. How did they get it?"

"No-see-ums got their name because they are so small, they're diffi-cult to see, but their bite is very painful."

"Are these flies you speak of the only blood feeding insects?"

"A few other types of insects feed on blood, too, like certain true bugs and fleas. There are even types of moths that suck blood. The type of parasite you run into often depends on the type of habitat you're in.

"There are also ticks and mites. Of course, they're related to the spi-ders and scorpions because they have eight legs in their adult form. We in-sects only have six. Also, their life cycle is quite different from ours. Most of the biting flies have to deposit their eggs in or near water. Ticks and mites deposit their eggs on land."

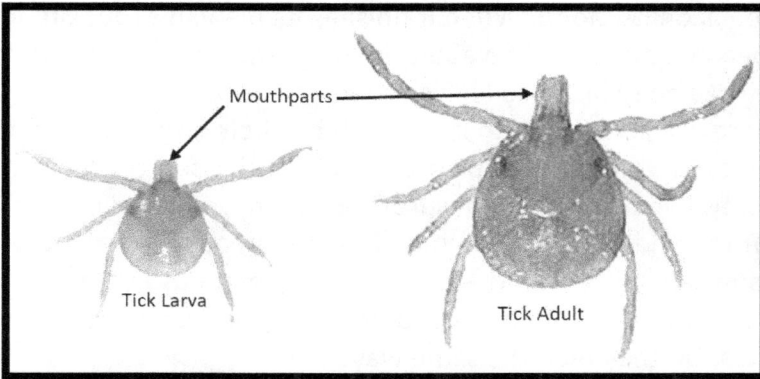

Ticks. On the left, the larval stage has three pairs of legs. It usually parasitizes small animals to get its blood meal. On the right, the adult has eight legs. It usually gets on a larger animal for its blood meal. At times, ticks sometimes transmit diseases from one individual to another when it feeds.

Jason asked, "What are some other ways that they're different, mosquito?"

Female ticks feed on animals that are called their hosts. Males do not feed for long, and their bodies never become inflated like those of females. Left, a female that has not fed on a host. Right, a female that has completed feeding on a host. Her inflated condition is usually referred to as engorged.

"It varies, depending on what you're talking about. Let's talk about the tick first. When a young tick hatches out of its egg, it only has six legs, like insects. They attach to a small animal, like a mouse or rat and feed on its blood for a while. Then they drop off and molt their skin to become a nymph. The nymph has eight legs, but it's not yet an adult.

"The nymph finds another animal, usually a larger one, like a dog or cat, and feeds on its blood. When it finishes its meal, it drops off and molts again to become an adult. The adult finds yet another animal and feeds on it. Female ticks need blood to lay eggs too.

There are some ticks that just stay on their host and go through all their life stages without dropping off, but most ticks go through all the stages, just as I've described. I'm surprised you haven't had one on you out here in nature. They're quite common in some areas.

Jason said, "I've had them crawling on me, but I've never had one suck blood from me. I found them before they started to feed. You mentioned mites. Do they feed the same way?"

"Mites are a little different. Of course, there are many different kinds of mites. Most of them are very small, and many parasitic mites live in or on an animal's skin. Maybe you've heard of skin conditions like scabes. An animal can lose its hair if scabes mites infest their skin.

"The most common type of parasitic mite you humans run into is one you call the chigger. It has a more complicated life than most. You see, the adult chigger, which has an orange or reddish color and is large enough to see with the human eye, is a predator on insects. When it lays its eggs on the ground, the young hatch into an immature stage called a larva. Larvae are so small they can't be seen without a microscope. They then look for an animal to jump on.

"Once they latch onto an animal, they produce some chemicals that dissolve the animal's skin, making a hole in it. The chigger larva sinks down into the hole and lives there for a few days, feeding on dissolved tissue. This is when people feel an itching sensation in their skin, and a little bump forms over the larva. Once the chigger larva has fed there for a few days, it leaves the skin and drops to the ground.

"It molts its skin, eventually becomes an adult, and then goes into its new life as an insect predator. Most people attacked by these mites think they get a chigger bite, but it's not a bite at all. They live in their skin until they have finished their meal."

"That's very interesting, mosquito, but let's get back to you. Is it true," Jason asked, "that you sometimes produce a disease when you bite us?"

"Actually, we don't produce diseases except for skin irritations and some reactions to our saliva when we feed, but it sometimes appears that we do. What happens is this. When we feed on certain animals, humans in-cluded, and we suck up their blood, some of the animals already have dis-eases. Of course, we don't know that when we feed.

"When we suck up their blood, we also suck up the parasites that are causing their disease, such as bacteria and other very small organisms. Then, if we don't complete our blood meal on that animal and have to go to an-other one to get more blood, we transfer the parasite to the next animal. It's not really our fault, but such relationships between the animals we feed on, their internal parasites, and us have been going on for millions of years, and their life cycles have become very complex."

Jason asked, "What do you mean?"

"Take malaria, for instance. That's a disease that affects millions of humans around the world. You don't usually find the disease in the United States any more, but it's found in many other countries, especially tropical ones.

"When we suck up the malarial parasites and transfer them to an-other animal, they enter the blood of the new animal and attack their tis-sues. Then, the parasites get into the blood and attack their red blood cells. They're able to live by feeding off of them, and they're able to reproduce there.

"When they reproduce, they cause the animal to have chills, and they become weak. This is very dangerous for the animal because they need their red blood cells to stay alive. It's the red blood cells in your body that deliver all the oxygen to your tissues.

"Once the parasite has been in that animal for a while, it produces a stage that circulates in the blood and can be picked up by a new mosquito. When they feed, there are more changes in the parasite within the mosquito before it is injected into another animal. It's a very complicated life cycle.

"It's usually a mosquito that transmits diseases like this, and, of course, there are other diseases, as well. Some other types of flies transmit some diseases, but it's usually in tropical countries where the diseases are poorly controlled.

"Wow, this is incredible." said Jason. "I had no idea how complex the life cycles of these tiny animals are. I guess you could say that their habitat is in our blood. So, while there are all the kinds of habitats out in nature, they also exist inside animals, too. Is that right?"

"Yes, you're right, but life cycles and parasites exist in and on plants, too. Believe it or not, all animals and plants have their parasites. It's a complicated world, so don't blame us for causing you some discomfort when we feed. That's our way of life, and we have to do it or we die.

"Of course, we have our enemies too. Many insects, like dragonflies, eat us, as well as some birds. Our larvae also get eaten in the water by fish and some types of aquatic insects. I think you'd find that we are the food for many other types of animals.

"We also risk our lives when we're trying to get our blood meal. We could get swatted by the animal in the process. When you look at how we live, it's a wonder we can ever grow up to be adults."

"You've been a very big help," Jason said. You've shown me things that I didn't know existed, and I'll certainly appreciate why parasites do the things they do. I guess you're just like most animals. You live off of something else. We live by eating plants and animals, and so do you. You just do it in a different way."

"Thanks for understanding," the mosquito said. "I'd better be off now. Because of your blood, I can now go and deposit my eggs. Thanks for the meal."

⑰

The Water Snake

As Jason left the swamp, he realized he got through it without a single leech, and the only parasites he had to contend with were a few mosquitoes that took some of his blood. He now had a new respect for them, but whether they needed blood to lay their eggs or not, he swatted at them whenever they tried to feed.

Just as he felt he was free of the pesky parasites, a deer fly began to circle his head, apparently looking for a spot to settle down for a quick blood meal. Jason swatted at it, and eventually it flew away to get its blood from an animal that was less defensive.

He moved out into the open, feeling a fresh breeze blowing off the lake. When he looked into the sky, he saw hundreds of dragonflies flying back and forth overhead. They were apparently searching for a meal, and he couldn't help but wonder how many mosquitoes and other biting flies they were catching.

By this time, he was by the lake. As he worked his way around the edge, looking closely for any signs of life, he spotted a water snake and stopped abruptly. Not experiencing the fear he had when he first saw the blue racer, he looked at it for a few minutes and finally said, "Hi. What are you doing here, snake?"

The water snake suddenly grew to an enormous size. Evidently startled by Jason's sudden presence, he looked up, flicked his forked tongue out and said, "I'm a water snake and this is where I live."

"I'm surprised to see you." Jason said. "I didn't see you on my last trip down here. Where do you go when you're not out on the water?"

"I sometimes hide in holes, under things, or in logs, and I come out occasionally to get some sun and feed on things around the water."

"You don't eat other snakes like the king snake does, do you?"

"No, I eat things like frogs and fish. I also may eat a salamander once in a while."

Jason said, "Are you dangerous, by any chance?"

"No, of course not. There are some water snakes, called moccasins by you humans, that are dangerous, but most of us are harmless. We do have teeth that we can bite with, and it may be painful to the animal we bite, but it won't cause any lasting problems for them.

"Once in a while, someone will think we're a moccasin because when we're alarmed, we sometimes flatten our head and body out and look like them. We don't really want to hurt anyone, though, and we prefer just to be left alone to live our life in peace and look for food."

Jason said, "I guess you hold some sort of position in your habitat like all the other animals do. Am I correct in assuming this?"

"Yes, you are," said the snake. "Everything is part of the food chain, you know. My part starts with the sun and plants, just like everyone else's. I can explain it all if you want me to.

"Sure. I'd like that. I've heard it before, but it can't hurt to hear it again." said Jason.

"Okay, here goes. Plants make food with sunlight, carbon dioxide gas in the air, and water. I think you humans call this process photosynthesis. It also gets nutrients from the soil. I think you already know this, but like you said, it's important to repeat because most life on earth depends on it.

"Insects of all sorts feed on the plants, and animals in the various habitats eat them as well. There are different food chains that branch off from that.

"When the insects enter my habitat, frogs and fish eat them, and I eat the frogs and fish. You see, one way to look at it is this. The energy that the sun passes on to the plants in the form of light to use to build their bodies ends up going up all the different food chains in our environment, all the way to the end. It's pretty remarkable when you think about it.

"I'm sure you understand that it's the sun that starts it all. If we didn't have the sun, none of this would happen. The plants wouldn't be able to make their food. The insects wouldn't have plants to feed on, and we would all suffer. The sun is the ultimate source of all this energy.

"While I don't like to talk about it, another snake, like the king snake, and some types of fish sometimes attempt to eat us. We're especially vulnerable to predation when we're young and small.

"There are also birds, like herons, egrets and hawks that eat us once in a while. Certain mammals, like raccoons and weasels, can eat us as well.

"As with most animals in nature, we have to be very careful or we could lose our life. That's why I flatten my head and body and sometimes hiss at anyone I think might harm me. I try to make myself as mean looking as I can to warn them so they'll leave me alone."

"I guess living out here is tough sometimes." Jason said. "What do you do when you're not hiding of feeding?"

"Once in a while, I'll find a mate and have some offspring. We don't lay eggs like many snakes do, you know. We have live young."

Jason asked, "What do your babies do when they're born? Do you take care of them like we humans do?"

"No, we don't. When our babies are born, they may hang around for a short while, and then they just go off on their own to look for small frogs and fish to eat. They grow up pretty fast, so if they don't get eaten by something else, they may double or triple their size within a year."

"That's pretty fast growing," Jason said. "If I'd grow that fast, I'd be as tall as a tree."

"There are some snakes, like pythons, that coil around their eggs until they hatch. That's about all the care any young snakes ever get. Even then, when they hatch, they're pretty much on their own."

Jason wrinkled his head, thinking about how different animals care for their young, and said, "What about other reptiles? Do any of them care for their young?"

"Not really," said the snake. "Turtles care for their young to some degree by digging holes and placing their eggs in them, and then they cover the eggs up so they're protected from predation. They don't stay and protect the eggs after that though.

"Alligators and other crocodile-like animals construct a nest and protect it from predators. If they catch someone by their nest, they'll even attack them. Hold on for just a minute."

Before Jason could respond, the water snake coiled its head back and lunged at a fish that was swimming by, and for the next few minutes it moved its head from side to side until the fish moved deeper into its mouth and almost appeared to slip down its throat.

Jason said, "Wow, I've never seen that before. You just ate that fish whole. How do you do that?"

"Well," the snake said, "I don't have teeth to chew with. All my teeth are sharp and pointed. With sharp and pointed teeth, I can hold on to my prey.

"When I eat, I grab the prey, a fish in this case, with my sharp teeth to hold on. Then I release the teeth on one side of my mouth to get a grip further up its body, and I keep alternating the sides of my mouth until I have pulled it completely inside.

"Once the fish is in my throat, I wiggle my body to help push the fish down, and once it's down far enough, I can eat again.

"There are a lot of snakes that constrict their prey before they eat it. King snakes, rat snakes, boa constrictors, and pythons are examples of those that are well known for their ability to constrict. They do this to kill their prey, and they swallow it in the same manner that I described when I eat a fish."

Jason said, "I've really enjoyed talking to you, but I think I'll leave you to catching some food and start heading back to the house. I've taken enough of your time. I wish you good luck."

"You, too," said the snake, "and thanks for caring about us."

⑱

The Fish

While walking along the water's edge, Jason saw swirling circles of activity and the occasional splashing of fish breaking through the water's surface. He watched periodic dorsal fins of large fish break the surface in their attempt to catch the frantic smaller fish that were scattering, even jumping out of the water to get to safety. As the schools broke into smaller groups and headed in different directions, their chasers moved along behind them until they once again became submerged.

As he came to a shallow cove in the lake, he saw some rather large fish swimming close to shore. They must have been swimming in a school, he thought, because he could see multiple dorsal fins moving together. Strangely enough, when he moved closer to the water, one of the larger fish broke away from the school, poked its head out of the water and looked directly at him.

Although this was enough to puzzle Jason, the fish appeared to actually be as interested in him as he was in the fish. It was just a moment before he swam over, raised his head out of the water again and said, "Hello. How are you, boy?"

Jason was astonished that the fish went to this trouble to speak to him, even though his day to this point had been one long series of conversations with animals that he wasn't supposed to be in communication with. Finally, he said, "I . . ., I'm fine. How about you?"

The fish said, "I'm fine, too. I'm just looking for a little food here, but pickings are pretty slim right now. When I saw you standing there, I thought you may be the type of person that would understand me. Am I correct in thinking this?"

Jason said, "Yes, I believe I am. I'm trying to learn about all the animals around here. I know you're a fish, but what kind of fish are you?"

"I'm a bass. I'm what you humans call a sport fish, and I live here in this lake. You may not see me often because I spend a lot of time down in holes and under tree branches where the water is cooler and the sun isn't so bright. I'm a little hungry right now, and that's why I'm up here near the top of the water. When I saw something of edible size go by, I wanted to check it out."

"But what type of food are you looking for?"

"We bigger fish feed mostly on insects and spiders, and sometimes we eat smaller fish. I'll also eat frogs and most anything that drops on top of the water or swims in my habitat. I'm really a predator. Is there anything in particular you'd like to know about us?"

"Oh, I'm just trying to learn whatever I can, so anything you tell me would be of value."

Jason looked closely at the fish and wondered if he had ever seen a bigger one in a lake like this. "You are a big fish," he said. "Is there anything you're afraid of?"

"There are a lot of things out here that we, as fish, are afraid of. Since I'm a large fish, as you put it, I have less to worry about than my younger friends. It's the smaller fish that have to worry more about predation."

Jason asked, "Why is that?"

"When we lay our eggs, they are in plain view of other living things in the water. Other fish and insects feed on them. Even newts may eat them on occasion. As we grow up, many fish, birds, and insects feed on us until we get big enough to scare them away. Finally, when we get large enough, the other things in the water have to fear us.

"That's when we're able to feed on many of the types of things that at one time we feared being eaten by. It's a long, hard existence from the time our eggs are deposited until we're large predators."

Jason said, "With all that predation, how do the young fish protect themselves?"

"Immediately after our eggs hatch, the young fish attempt to stay in areas of the lake that have vegetation in which to hide. If they don't have vegetation to hide in, they have very little chance of survival.

"It's after hatching that our numbers become very high, but shortly after that, our numbers dwindle. Besides the predatory fish and insects that are in the water, there are alligators in some of the southern lakes, and many birds, like herons, egrets, anhingas, and cormorants that feed upon us. It's a really big time for them.

"Then, as their bellies get full with all the young fish, they begin their nesting season, and it's easy for them to find enough food to feed their young. You see, our cycles are kind of coordinated, and knowing that predation is usually high at that time of the year, we actually produce more offspring than the lake can support, but when predation is all finished, our numbers are just about where they should be."

Jason said, "I don't understand. You say you produce more offspring than you need? I've heard this from some of the other animals, but why do you do that? Why not just produce the number you need in the first place?"

"You say you've heard it before. That's because all animals do it. They produce more offspring than their habitat can hold because of the predation and diseases that can knock their numbers down.

This is a survival strategy, and it all works toward a balance of nature. Look at it this way. If we didn't produce such a high number of eggs, all the things that feed on us wouldn't have the food they need to grow and reproduce. Each animal in the food chain is dependent upon the things they eat for their own survival.

"Sometimes, this overproduction backfires on us, but it usually happens when our populations are tampered with. For instance, if predators in our population are taken away, the numbers of animals they normally eat may become too large because of this overproduction, and diseases usually end up wiping many of them out.

I guess what I'm saying is that there is a delicate balance between the predators and their prey, and anything that upsets that balance causes the populations to change in ways that are harmful to the plants and animals that remain.

"In my environment, upsetting a population of fish isn't the end to the problem. As I've indicated, it fits in with the food chain concept that I'm sure you have been learning about from all the animals you have talked with. It takes years to establish a balance like the one I'm talking about, and one little change can upset the entire food chain."

"It seems very complicated," Jason said. "I always looked at predation as just something that happened. I didn't realize it was so important in nature's balance. In spite of its importance, I guess predation is one of your greatest fears when growing up."

"Actually," said the fish, "predation is something we expect in nature, and it's something we have to adjust to in our lives. "You can see this in most any population in the world, even in areas where there are very large populations of wild animals, like Africa.

"When you get out on the African plains and look at the extremely large populations of mammals there, you can understand why predators are needed to keep the populations in check. It's the same here in our lake, or anywhere else, for that matter.

"If you leave these populations alone, they will more-or-less stay in balance. As long as there are enough plants to eat, the land will support large populations of animals that eat plants, herbivores, as you humans call them. Whenever their populations get too large, the predator populations will flourish. If the herbivore populations get too low, the predator populations dwindle. That's how nature works.

"I have greater fears than predation, though. What I fear most are humans."

Jason asked, "What do you mean? Are you afraid of fishermen, or what?"

"It's not so much that I'm afraid to get hooked. Many fishermen that catch us these days release us back into the environment, and we appreciate that. That's a lot better than ending up in someone's frying pan, but, speaking for our entire population and all the other things that live in an aquatic environment, I have fears much greater than that.

"You see, humans represent a dominant form of life on earth. They can do just about anything they want to do, and they have the power to alter the environment in any way they see fit.

"There are more and more humans that are taking many of the habitats for themselves and causing the habitats of many animals on the land to change. When changes occur on land, they often change our habitat also.

"What they do most is cause changes in the water that enters our habitat, and this sometimes causes us to be unhealthy. Some chemicals can enter our lake and even kill us. They also can kill the things we eat. Others may cause us to have problems with reproducing, and it's something we can't control. If we're going to survive, it's really up to you humans to stop allowing toxic things to get into our water.

"It's not only for us, you know. When our water gets polluted, the water also will get back to humans when they run it into their homes. Polluted water is bad for everyone."

"Thanks for the information." Jason said. "You've opened my eyes to some of the important things I have to think about. When I become a biologist, maybe I can work on some of these things and make the world a safer and better place to live.

"I apologize for the things we have done to make your life miserable. I think if people knew what they were doing, they would think more about how to avoid polluting the environment.

"It seems to me that what everyone out here is telling me is that everything in nature is important, and that we humans have been irresponsible by not doing our share to keep the balances of nature going as it should be. If we don't think about it, we will suffer in the long run. Our lack of concern will backfire on us. I'll try to let everyone know about what you said."

"Thank you," the fish said. "I'm glad I met you. You've given me and the populations that live around me some hope."

"It's my pleasure," said Jason. "I hate to end our conversation, but it's getting late, and I have to get home. Good luck with everything."

"Good luck to you too," he said, and he swam into deeper water.

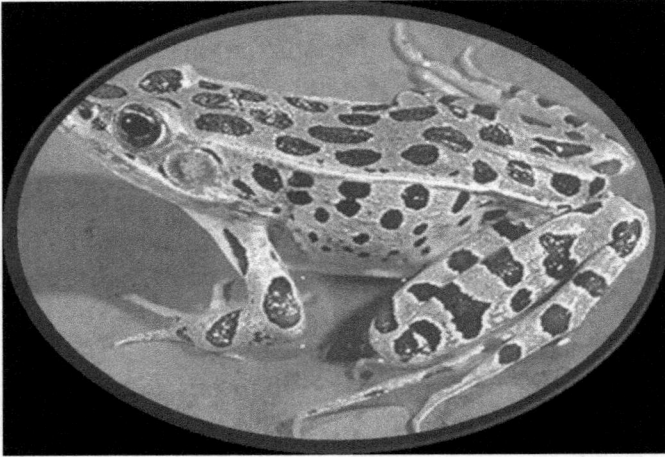

⑲

The Frog

As Jason walked along, he had a lot to think about. While he was thrilled to learn about all the animals and was finally beginning to understand how nature works, he was now worried about the plants and all of the animals he had met. Somehow, he was going to have to learn even more so he could understand the intricate relationships between every

118

living thing in nature. Then, with that knowledge, he would attempt to convince everyone about how important it is to respect all these things and the places in which they live.

Just as he was finishing his discussion with the fish and was in deep thought about the future of the animals, a frog jumped out of the water and landed at his feet. Immediately, the frog pushed its front end up with its feet and looked at him as though he was waiting for Jason to say something.

But before Jason got a word in, the frog's body began to grow, and within a few seconds, it was just as big as he was. He blinked his big, round eyes, gave out a croak and said, "Hi, young man. How are you on this nice day?"

"I'm fine," said Jason. "How about you?"

"Oh, things are about usual."

Jason said, "Well, you're a very handsome frog. Who exactly are you, and what are you doing here?"

The frog said, "I'm a leopard frog. You can tell this by my body shape, the size of my body, my large eyes, the spots on my back and the small pads on my toes. I'm sorry I almost jumped on you, but I was sitting at the edge of the water, and a fish suddenly came up and tried to eat me. All I wanted to do was get out of there."

"I can understand that." said Jason, agreeing with the frog. "It must be tough living as a frog out here."

"Yes, it is. I have a lot of problems. There are a lot of animals that want to eat me, no matter where I go, and I have to be especially careful." The frog carefully looked around.

"What are some of the animals that try to eat you?" Jason asked.

The frog gave out another croak and seemed to be getting his thoughts together. Finally, he said, "The most important predators I have found around the water are fish and snakes, but larger frogs try to eat us smaller guys at times. When I venture away from the water, there are a number of other snakes, birds, and mammals that want to eat me. Birds like herons and egrets are especially fond of eating frogs like me. I don't have a place to go that is completely safe."

Jason noticed a sad look on the frog's face.

"Some of my friends go up in trees, but they also spend a lot of time on low vegetation and on the ground. I can't be away from water for long periods of time because my skin dries out if it doesn't get wet occasionally. I breathe through my skin, and this can't work very well unless my skin is damp."

Jason asked, "You mean all the air you breathe goes through your skin?"

"Oh, no, not all of it. Most of what I breathe in goes through my nose, but some gases go through my skin as well. It may be interesting to you to know that breathing through my nose is a little different than yours."

"How's that?" Jason had an intent look on his face.

Frog with its dewlap expanded. It breathes by expanding its dewlap with air pulled in through its nostrils, and then it contracts certain muscles associated with its dewlap, forcing the air into its lungs. Developing frogs, tadpoles, breathe through gills.

"When you humans breathe, your chest and abdominal muscles function to enlarge your chest cavity, and that sucks in air through your nose and mouth. When we breathe, we enlarge a bubble of skin beneath our chin (a dewlap) to pull in air. If you look closely, you can see the bubble puffing up and down under our chin. When we force the bubble to get smaller, it pushes air into our lungs."

"Wow. That is different! I never really thought much about how frogs breathe.

"You know, Mr. Frog, I haven't seen many of your kind out here. I didn't see any when we came here on our earlier trip. How come you're out here now?"

"You probably didn't see us because we are usually trying to hide during the day. Much of our activity is at night. I'm out here attempting to catch some food. I didn't get enough last night. I eat mostly insects and spiders, but I'll occasionally eat other things, as long as they are small enough.

"It's at night that we do other things as well, especially if it rains a lot. We do our singing mostly after a rain so we can find a mate and lay our eggs in the water. It's after a rain that the air is moist, and we can hop around and find new spots to visit without worrying about drying out.

"It is during our mating season that I sing my songs most. Our songs help us to tell other frogs where we are, and it also helps us attract a mate. Every frog around the lake is singing when the conditions are right."

Jason was amazed by what the frog had told him, and he asked, "But how do you know where your mate is if everyone is singing at the same time?"

"Good question, young man! Let me try to explain it. I'm a southern leopard frog. There are other kinds of frogs around, like gray tree frogs, squirrel tree frogs, pine woods tree frogs, barking tree frogs, bull frogs, cricket frogs, and others. There are other types as well. The way that we know if a mate is like us is that we all have a particular call, and we can tell the difference between them. I pick a mate that looks and calls like me.

"Once the eggs that we deposit in the water hatch, there are tadpoles everywhere. That's what we call our young."

Jason asked, "You say you lay your eggs in the water? What happens after they hatch? How do they breathe?" Jason now realized that this was something new to think about.

"When our eggs hatch and the little tadpoles swim out, they begin eating vegetation and different things at the bottom of the water. They breathe their air through gills like fish do or they swim up to the top of the water and gulp some air through the surface of the water.

"As they feed, they get larger and eventually grow legs. When they are big tadpoles, they get closer to the edge of the water, their legs get larger, they lose their tail and gills and they begin to breathe air through their nose and skin just like I do. By the following year, they are ready to mate and lay their own eggs.

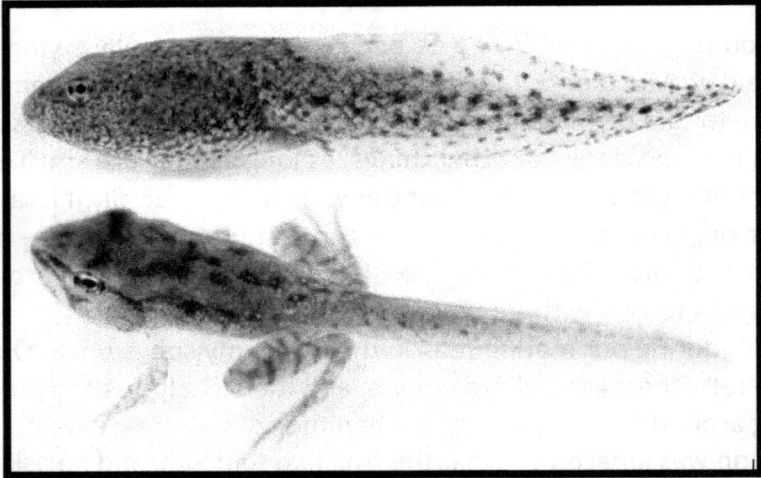

Most frogs deposit their eggs in freshwater ponds and lakes. The pictures above show two stages in the development of tadpoles. The early form (top picture) must transform into an adult before it leaves the water. The later form (bottom picture) has developed legs and is about to leave its aquatic form.

Shaking its head, the frog continued. "I'll tell you something you may not know. Being a frog is a hard life, and it starts even before we hatch. Fish, birds and insects eat both our eggs and tadpoles in the water, and when young frogs come out of the water, all those other things that I told you about feed on them. We're lucky if we can survive long enough to lay our eggs.

"Some of my relatives have it worse. Bull frogs are very large as frogs go, and humans sometimes catch them for food. Personally, I would rather be a leopard frog.

The frog looked sadly at Jason and quietly stated, "But that's not the worst of it. Humans cause us more problems. Environmental pollution is causing our numbers to drop."

"Why is that?" asked Jason with great concern in his voice.

"We are very sensitive to changes in our environment. I overheard what the fish was saying to you. He's right about pollution. Our problem is that if any of these pollutants get on our skin, we get sick and sometimes die."

Jason asked, "Is that why I don't see as many frogs as I used to?"

"That's one of the very important reasons. Our skin is very sensitive to chemicals. I guess it's safe to say that harmful chemicals are our most important threat. People use pesticides on everything. They spray their plants and even their houses. When we land on these chemicals, we absorb them through our skin. Can you do anything for us?"

Jason quickly replied, "Well, I can try. I'm going to study real hard and learn as much as I can about our environment, and I'll tell everyone about how we have to keep our environment clean."

"That would be a very nice thing to do," said the frog happily. "Maybe there's a chance for our populations to survive and even get bigger. Well, I'm going to be on my way. Thanks for caring about us."

"It's my pleasure, frog. I'll look for you the next time I'm down here."

⑳

An Unexpected Meeting

As Jason began to meander back toward the house, he took a different path and passed through a small section of another woodland area. Surprisingly, there were no large insects or other animals to draw his attention, making him wonder about all the associations he had developed with the natural world on his trip from the house. It was real, he thought. It wasn't every day one had a chance to commune with nature as he had done, but his adventures were apparently coming to an end, and he began to have strange feelings about them.

On the one hand, he felt some disappointment that his field trip was coming to an end, especially since it included some very enjoyable and educational conversations with the animals. And since the entire trip was so bizarre, he was beginning to wonder if it had happened at all.

In certain other ways, he felt extremely good about the experiences he had, and he wondered how many other people had learned and understood what he now knew about nature. He turned and looked around, hoping to see some of his new friends, but they were nowhere in sight. He toyed with the idea of walking back through some of the areas he had just come from and searching for some of his new friends, but it was getting late, and he knew he'd better head for the house. Maybe he could go on a similar trip on another day.

While still in a dream world, he slowly walked and thought about these things that had happened to him, he entered an area in which a thick mist had settled over the forest community, making it eerie and difficult to see the path except that which was directly in front of him. He was especially worried about this because he had never been in this section of the forest before, and it was possible for him to lose his way.

Through the thickening mist, he heard a faint haunting sound that added to the mystique. It was the sound of what appeared to be a Native American flute, playing a tune that was more beautiful than anything he had ever heard. It was as though the sounds of the flute were coming from Mother Nature herself, and as he walked toward the source, the sounds became more pronounced.

He began to look around in an attempt to determine the origin of the music and to be sure he was following the path closely, and suddenly he saw what appeared to be someone sitting on a log beside the path just ahead of him. While initially nervous, he wondered who this could be, and as he approached, he noticed it was a boy about his age, holding a flute in his hand. This, at least, solved the problem of where the beautiful sounds were coming from, but he remained confused about the reason for his being here.

Jason noticed that the boy was wearing a head band with a feather in it, and he was dressed in leather clothing. His hair was black and straight. Judging from what he had read in his books, he recognized him as a Native American boy.

His first thought, of course, was *what is he doing here*. He had not

125

seen anyone like this since he had come to stay with his aunt and uncle, and he wasn't aware that Indians currently lived in these parts. Nevertheless, it was a pleasant surprise, and he was very interested in asking him some questions. After all, who would be better to learn about nature from.

Kokopelli was a Native American who traveled over great distances and played a flute. His figure is found carved on large rocks in the Western United States.

When Jason approached the boy, he stopped and gazed at him momentarily, and the boy, apparently also interested in him, returned the gaze. Just as he was about to speak, the boy spoke first.

"Hi." he said. "Are you Jason?"

"Why yes, I am. How do you know my name, and who are you?"

"My name is Little Eagle, and I've been waiting here to speak with you."

"Speak with me?" Jason asked.

"Yes, I have heard that you are interested in the animals and plants here, and I would like to tell you what they have meant to us. My tribe lived here many years ago, and we had an approach to nature that I think you would be interested in."

Jason said, "I would very much like to hear about what these things mean to you, but isn't it the same as what it means to me?"

"I'm not sure what the animals and plants mean to you, but from what I've heard, you are serious about learning about their lives, and this interests me very much too. You see, Jason, many people today do not have the interest that you have, and it is because of this that we should talk.

"My people lived a life that was very close to nature. Some of our people that live today still practice this way of life, although it's becoming

126

very difficult to do in a modern world. We depended on many plants and animals for our lives, and we learned as much as we could about these things. We respected all things in nature, both the living and the non-living.

Even though Jason had a puzzled look on his face, Little Eagle continued. "Many people today have lost this respect for nature, and they think we must dominate the entire earth without caring about nature and our rapidly changing and deteriorating environments. While we did eat the animals and plants in our environment, we thought of all living things as our equals, and we understood that these things can also be our teachers."

Jason's puzzled look grew more visible, and he quickly blurted out, "Wait a minute, Little Eagle. What do you mean when you say respect living and non-living parts of nature?"

Little Eagle answered, "While I believe you do respect the living things around you, Jason, you should realize that the non-living things, like rocks, soil, water, and air provide important things for nature that living things depend upon. That's why I say we should respect all parts of nature."

Jason looked at Little Eagle, still with a confused expression on his face, and asked, "How do rocks provide important things for us?"

"Well," said Little Eagle, "there are several ways to look at it. First, rocks that are part of our Mother Earth are in many forms. We can look at a rock and tell if it has developed from volcanoes, changes that have come about over millions of years, or from deposits over long periods of time. Sometimes, they even include the bodies of plants and animals that died millions of years ago. These rocks represent the history of the earth, and they are part of our history.

"Rocks, which contain a large variety of chemicals, are cracked and further broken down over time by changes in temperature and certain chemicals, and they are eroded by wind and rain so that they eventually form soil. The chemicals that are locked in these rocks become available to bacteria and other tiny living things in the soil, and they help make these chemicals available to plants. Many of these chemicals provide nutrients for plants to grow.

Jason asked, "But what about the water and air you mentioned a few minutes ago?"

Little Eagle answered, "One of the interesting things about our planet is that it has air that animals and plants can breathe and water that is important to our lives. We are so lucky to be on a planet like this, a planet that provides all the things we need for life. If it wasn't for these things, life on our planet would be either non-existent or of a form that is quite different from what we know.

"Air should be clean so that we and all the other living things won't breathe in toxic chemicals. Toxic air sometimes comes naturally from things like fires and volcanic activity, but most of it comes from pollution that develops from cars and trucks, as well as industrial wastes. Without clean air, we and our brothers and sisters in the animal and plant world develop sickness. This is true for the water as well.

"Water, like air, is very important to all living things. The chemicals in both air and water are important to the growth and development of our bodies. If toxic chemicals enter our bodies by way of unclean water and air, we become sick and may die.

"This is part of the reason for the extinction of many plants and animals today. While extinction is sometimes a natural occurrence in the world, just like the rise of new types of animals and plants, extinction is occurring more rapidly today than in the past because of toxic substances in the air and water. Plants and animals are sometimes not able to tolerate these toxic materials. Some people are even saying that the amount of extinction on our earth is becoming so high that it almost is equivalent to the period of time that occurred sixty-five million years ago when the dinosaurs died.

"Plants are our friends, Jason. They often filter out toxic materials and help clean the air and water, but they often die from them as well, and many of the trees in the world are dying because of it. Also, humans are continuously logging forested areas and removing the trees that we need to help clean the air. As populations of humans grow, they will remove more and more of the trees until there are very few left.

"Some people think that trees are only important to build things with, but this is probably one of their least important features. Trees and other plants and their place in nature are important as living creatures for our survival.

"Plants that live in the water function in a similar manner. Water distributes both good and bad chemicals to living things, and many of the toxins that result from pollution run off the land into ponds, lakes, rivers, streams, and oceans during rains and are removed from the water by aquatic plants. Just like the plants on land, they represent a type of environmental filter. However, when these toxins become abundant, they also kill aquatic plants and the animals that feed upon them, adding to the pollution of our water. When we drink this water, we suffer too.

"Also, many of these toxic chemicals in water enter animals in food chains and often end up being stored in the animals' bodies. When we humans and other animals eat them, we often get these toxins and sometimes store them in our bodies. They may end up causing us to have poor health in one way or another."

Jason remarked, "I guess we've gotten ourselves in a mess over the years. Did your people understand this when you lived here?"

Little Eagle answered, "There is much we can learn from nature, and if you read about how we lived in the past, I think you will find that nature was a very important part of everything we did. Our religion, the origins of many things we knew about, and our very lives depended on our relationship with nature.

"Just as you have been learning about the different animals and plants that live here, we also learned about them and knew of their importance. We understood that everything is related and are part of our universe. We often formed stories to pass down through our generations that told about these things, so that our children and their children understood the importance of nature.

Jason said, "Times are changed from when you lived here, Little Eagle. Life now is a lot different from life in those days. Many people now feel that we no longer need nature in our lives."

Understanding what Jason said, Little Eagle answered, "Many people today are unhappy with their lives, and they have lost respect for many things. Even you and I, although of different times and societies, are brothers in this universe. My elders would tell you that we must look at things this way and rekindle the love and respect for one another, including ourselves, other people, the animals, plants, and the things that our earth is made of. We must find a balance. This is just as important today as it was when we lived here.

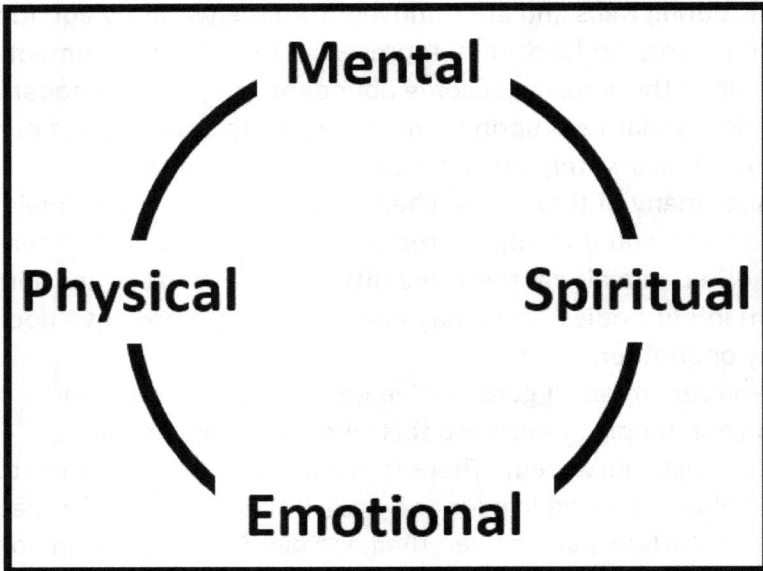

The circle of life, as shown in this figure, means many things to the people who use them, including the path one must follow to be the best they can be, balancing the different forces in their lives.

"As my elders have pointed out, we must walk the magic circle together, experience different things in life and learn about the ways of all living things. Without a sincere interest in our surroundings, they would tell you that we are sure to leave the magic circle and become lost."

"What's this magic circle you speak about, Little Eagle? I read something about it in one of my books, but I can't remember what it is."

"The magic circle means many things. In some ways, it represents the path we follow in life, Jason. It is a plan for life, for learning and becoming aware of our position in life, and it is related to many of the things you have learned about nature. We must follow this circle and experience what life has to offer and appreciate others that are in different positions in this circle. If you follow this path properly, you will eventually learn more about yourself, the people you meet, and about nature. You should find a book in your library that discusses this circle and follow it throughout your life."

Jason realized the wisdom in what Little Eagle said, and he managed to slip in a comment. "People where I live know very little about nature, and it seems like they sometimes aren't even interested in learning about it."

"Ah, yes." Little Eagle said. "That's one of the modern world's greatest problems. They no longer have this connection my elders and I have spoken about. The balance humans once had in their life has vanished in many of them. My elders have said that many of the problems that have arisen in today's human populations, like lack of respect, stress and lack of direction, have come about because they have lost touch with nature.

"Look at all you've learned by talking to the animals and observing them in nature. By closely examining their lives, you've learned that they all fill a particular place in nature. There is an important relationship between all of them, and they often depend on this relationship for their survival

"These different animals and plants develop food chains, starting with plants that get their energy from the sun and make their own food with carbon dioxide gas and nutrients from the soil. Plants also give off oxygen that animals breathe in, and plants use oxygen too.

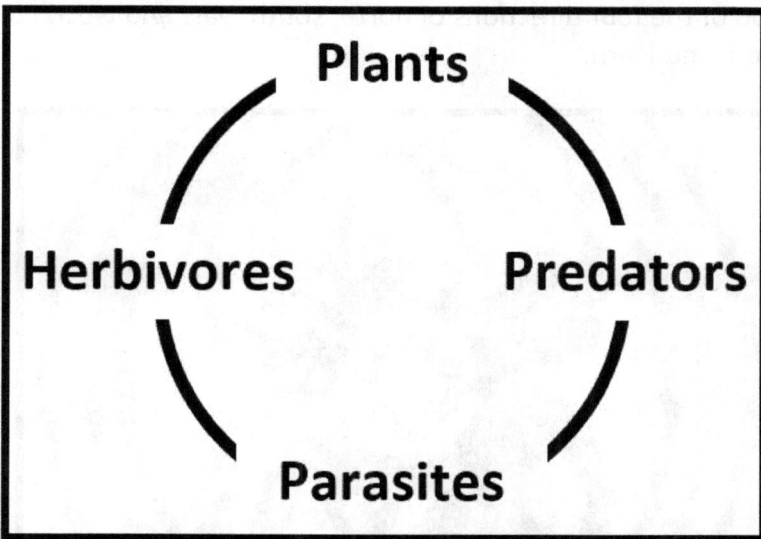

Plants

Herbivores

Predators

Parasites

There is a most important balance between organisms in a natural environment, providing the populations of these organisms are left alone to interact with each other. Upsetting these conditions and the balance is lost.

"Certain animals, the herbivores, eat these plants and others, the carnivores, feed on them. Within the various habitats, these food chains become very complex. These associations become even more complex when we include cycles involving such animals as parasites. Their lives are inter-twined into another very important circle of life.

"There is no doubt about the closeness of living things in the natural world, and it is evident throughout these food chains. What we all should remember is that the human animal is a member of these communities.

"Please don't forget about these things, Jason, as many others have done. Learn from the experiences you have had here, and make an attempt to teach others what you have learned."

At this time, Little Eagle removed a pendant from around his neck and said, "You are my brother, Jason. I would like to give you this pendant to wear to remind you of our relationship, as well as nature and our respon-sibilities for protecting it. It is a symbol of a water spider who represents the bringer of fire. On the spider's back are two circles and a cross. Circles are important symbols that have meant many things to us. They will remind you of the earth and the magic circle that we talked about, and the cross will remind you of the four directions of north, south, east and west. Follow the circle, Jason, and learn."

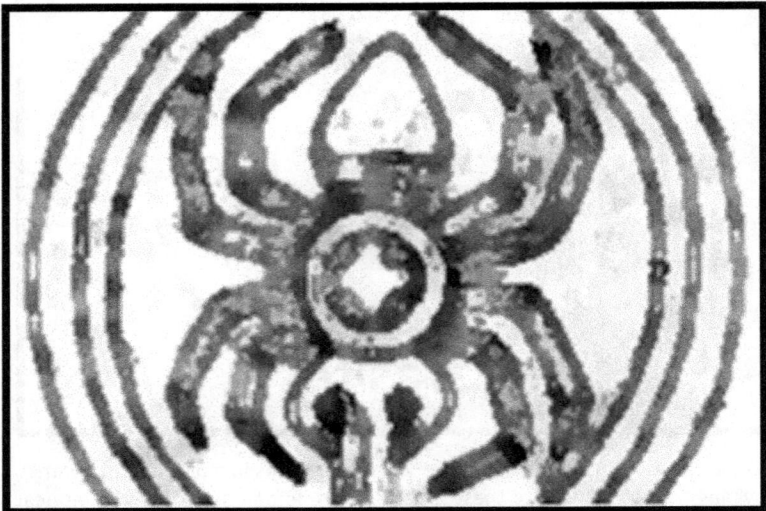

Encircling the water spider, a symbol of nature, are circles which remind certain groups of people about earth and its relationship with all life forms and the magic circle of life which one must follow as an important member of our ecosystems. The cross on the spider's back reminds of the four directions on the compass.

Jason was overwhelmed at receiving this amazing gift from Little Eagle. He thanked him from the bottom of his heart and reluctantly bid him goodbye. As he walked off with the pendant now around his neck, contemplating the things that Little Eagle had said, he noticed that the flute playing had resumed. Within moments, his walking had taken him to a point where the tune of nature faded, and the fog had lifted, and when he turned to wave a final goodbye to Little Eagle, his friend had vanished.

Like all of the other experiences he had that day, it was quickly becoming only a memory, but his memory of the events remained vivid in his mind. It was real, he thought. He turned again and began walking back to the house.

㉑

Back at the Farm

A s Jason thought about his adventure, the realization that all the different things in nature in one way or another have a connection repeated itself, and he now understood what happens when you change even a small part of it. *There's no doubt about it*, he thought. *Our environment is a very delicate and precious thing, and we must take special care of it*.

As quickly as he had fallen asleep the night before, his eyes popped open, and he once again stared at the ceiling. He was no longer in the field, talking with animals as large as himself or the Indian boy who he had happened upon. It was all a dream, he thought, or was it? The experiences were so real and the memories now so vivid that it left him confused.

He reached for the gift he had received from Little Eagle, and sure enough, the spider pendant hung around his neck. Did David or his aunt and uncle secretly give him the gift, or was it from Little Eagle? The mystery of his experiences now made him wonder even more. It somehow must have all happened.

In spite of his confused thoughts, he knew that somehow today was going to be different than any other day in his life. He knew that this day would be extraordinary because he now felt like he was an important part of everything he had experienced.

When he came downstairs for breakfast, he excitedly talked at length to David about the animals they had seen the previous day, and David, Aunt Sarah, and Uncle Ted listened attentively as Jason related every detail of what he remembered about nature. Their discussion lasted long after they had finished breakfast, and the entire family was amazed at how much Jason remembered from the trip they had made the day before.

David said, "I'm really impressed with your memory, Jason. You're going to be a great biologist one day. I'm surprised that you've remembered so much."

"Well," Jason said, "it's not all from yesterday." He hesitated to tell David what had happened but then said, "You see, I had some help."

David, intrigued with Jason's comment said, "What do you mean, Jason?"

"When I went to sleep last night, I couldn't get all the plants and animals out of my mind. All the things you told me kept bouncing around in my head, and I thought I'd never get to sleep. Before I knew it, I was out in the field again, but this time the animals were as big as I was, and I talked with them."

"Really?" David said. "And what did they say to you?"

"They said pretty much everything you had told me, but it was different."

"How's that?"

"It was like I was part of everything, and the animals and I understood each other. I really think I got to know them quite well."

David asked, "What do you feel is the most important lesson you learned from them?"

"I think the most important thing I learned is that the Earth and all the animals and plants are important, and that somehow, they all depend on one another. And they depend on us to keep the environment clean."

The Magic of Nature – H. R. Hermann

"That's right." David said. "It's a very complex system, and each part is important to the survival of the whole.

"And, you're right. We are an intimate part of the entire system, and it's important that we protect it. We must make every attempt to handle our wastes in such a manner that they don't pollute the environment. Otherwise, we and all of our animal friends will suffer in the long run.

"We also must understand that pollution not only affects our most immediate environment; it affects other habitats as well. While we can see the direct affects of dirty water on our environment, there are many things happening in the environment that have a more indirect relationship with it. Our dirty water and use of chemicals can affect animals that aren't even in the habitat that these changes originate in.

"Also, it is important to recycle what we can. There are so many people on our Earth that we are depleting it of its natural resources. Whenever we recycle glass, metals, paper, and other things, we are protecting these resources."

David said, "Jason, I notice that you're wearing a really neat pendant with a spider on it. It's very nice, but I didn't see you wearing it yesterday. Where did you get it?"

Jason quickly thought so that he chose his words very carefully and said, "It was a gift from a friend to remind me about nature. It represents the giving of fire, the Sun, the Earth and the magic circle of life. Along with the information you gave to me, they are my most valuable gifts, and I thank you for everything you've done."

David looked at Jason and smiled. It was a special day for both of them.

Jason spent the remainder of the week with David, each day walking out into nature and observing the plants and animals that he loved so much. He didn't have the dream again, but as far as he was concerned, the week that he spent in the country with his cousin, David, and his special time with nature and Little Eagle were the most important days of his life.

He returned to his house in the city as a different person, a person who was no longer isolated from the rest of the world, and he more fully understood that living in the city sometimes caused people to forget about nature. It was somewhat like his mother had said to him one time, "out of sight, out of mind."

136

Yet, just as food webs are present out in nature, they overlap into the lives of people who live in the cities. The food they eat, the buildings they build and the pleasures they experience, in one way or another, are tied to nature, and whatever goes on in nature will end up affecting everyone's life. Unfortunately, events in urban areas affect nature, as well, and we must be careful what we put into our environment. He now knew that no living animal was separate from others, not even humans that live far away from a natural environment.

Wherever he went, people commented on his beautiful pendant, and it gave him an opportunity to talk about his favorite things. And whenever he talked to someone, he shared his thought that it is everyone's responsibility to take care of the environment and the animals and plants that are part of it. He reminded them that it not only will save the creatures out in nature, it will help humans to live healthy lives as well.

Glossary

Amphibian – A group of vertebrate animals (animals with a backbone) that spend their immature lives in water and breathe by way of gills. Adults generally lose their gills and breathe through lungs and their skin, although there are many that spend their entire life in water. Examples of amphibians are frogs, toads, salamanders, and newts.

Ancestors – Ancestors are individuals who have come before. For instance, your great grandfathers and great-great grandmothers are examples of your ancestors. All animals and plants have ancestors that had offspring (children, in the case of humans), and their offspring had offspring as well. Sometimes, you or your parents can trace your ancestors back to another country where they were born.

Anole – Lizards in the family Polycridae. There are more than 250 species, most of which are found in the tropics, constituting the largest genus of lizards in the world. The only species of this family that is native to the continental United States is the Green Anole, *Anolis carolinensis*. Its range includes the states that border the Gulf of Mexico, from Texas to Florida, and the adjacent states of Georgia, South Carolina and North Carolina. It is most commonly found on fences, around old buildings, on shrubs and vines. There are several species that have been introduced to the United States, especially in Florida, from more tropical areas. See Peterson's Field Guide to the Reptiles and Amphibians by Roger Conant and Joseph T. Collins, published by Houghton Mifflin Company, for further information.

Antennae – A pair of long devices called antennae are found on the heads of many insects and other arthropods. They are sensory devices that are used for many reasons. There are small hairs on insect antennae that are sometimes sensitive to certain sounds and smells. In a way, the antennae are sometimes used like our ears and nose so that the insect can tell something about its environment.

Arthropods – Organisms that have an exoskeleton (external skeleton) and jointed appendages. Examples are insects, spiders, crabs, lobsters, crayfish, scorpions, ticks, mites, millipedes and centipedes.

Blue Birds – Blue birds are songbirds that have a large amount of blue color in their feathers. Two examples are regular blue birds that are found in many parts of the country and mountain blue birds that are just found in highland areas. Look them up on the internet and find out about their lives.

Breeding Season – Most wild animals have a particular time of the year for mating with one another. Birds are excellent examples of such animals because they develop breeding plumage which displays their most outstanding colors and patterns, usually during the Spring and early Summer. Males are generally the most colorful of the two sexes, and along with their colorful plumage, they display courtship behaviors which sometimes include particular songs and complex dances.

Community – A community is an area with its living (biotic) components, such as the animals and plants. It does not include the abiotic (non-living) components. Communities are usually combined with abiotic components (like air, soil, rocks and water) to form an ecosystem.

Corn Snake – The name corn snake was given to a type of snake that has a lot of red in its pattern. They are known to most herpetologists (people who study reptiles) as red rat snakes. There are many types of rat snakes (such as gray rat snake, Texas rat snake, black rat snake and yellow rat snake), but the red rat snake (or corn snake) is one of the most beautiful.

Daddy-Long-Legs – Many people believe that the daddy-long-legs is a type of spider, but it isn't. It's true that it is related to the spiders, but it really belongs to a different group of arthropods (things with an external skeleton and jointed legs). There are many stories about daddy-long-legs that are really not true. For instance, some people believe they are dangerous, but they're not. They don't bite, they don't have fangs like spiders, and they don't have venom glands that produce any type of venom. Therefore, they are completely harmless.

Dewlap – A dewlap (also dulap) is a device on the bottom of certain lizard's necks that can puff out when the lizard is attempting to express dominance behavior in its territory. There is a thin band made of cartilage in their throat that can be expanded by muscles when it wants to put its dewlap out. Dewlaps can be different colors, depending on the species of lizard that has it.

Eagle – Eagles are predatory birds that are very large and majestic. The eagles that we may see in the United States are the bald eagle and golden eagle. Both are large birds that prey on smaller land animals and fish. Their life styles are somewhat like hawks and falcons. The bald eagle is our national bird.

Eardrum – Our eardrum is in our ear, and it's made-up of a membrane that vibrates when sound waves hit it. Its movement is like a drum when you beat upon it. When it vibrates, the vibrations are transferred to tiny bones within our ear that wiggle and pass the message from sound waves to our inner ear and eventually to a nerve that goes to our brain. This is how we hear. Many animals have an eardrum, even insects. Insects hear in other ways as well. They have hairs on their antennae and body that may detect certain sounds, but they also may have a membrane somewhere on the body that functions in a similar way to our eardrum. The "eardrum" of insects can be on different parts of the body, depending on the species. For instance, eardrums on short-horned grasshoppers are on the sides of their first abdominal segment; eardrums of long-horned grasshoppers are on the tibia of their forelegs; eardrums of some moths and certain other insects may be on their thorax.

Ecosystem – An ecosystem is a combination of all biotic (living) and abiotic (non-living) things in a particular area. Examples of biotic components are the animals and plants that exist in an area. Abiotic components are things like rock, water, air and soil. The way we treat ecosystems is very important for the livelihood of the organisms that live there.

Egret – An egret is a type of wading bird, a bird that wades in the water or near the water's edge where it looks for food. They eat a variety of foods, such as frogs, fish, insects and even lizards and snakes. Their beaks are generally long and slender for catching their prey, and their feet are sometimes slightly webbed so that they can stand on aquatic vegetation. Two egrets that are commonly seen in the southeastern United States, and sometimes in other areas, are the Great White Egret and the Snowy Egret. Another common species which was introduced from other areas of the world is the Cattle Egret. While Cattle Egrets generally nest in areas by water, they forage in open fields and often follow cattle and other animals that walk in the grass and scare up insects, upon which the egrets feed.

Field Guides – An excellent way to identify reptiles and amphibians is to use a book like *A Field Guide to Reptiles and Amphibians* by Roger Conant and Joseph T. Collins, published by Houghton Mifflin Company. The National Wildlife Federation's *Field Guide to Insects and Spiders of North America* by Arthur V. Evans, published by Sterling Publishing Company, is excellent for arthropods. *The Sibley Field Guide to Birds* by David Allen Sibley is an excellent bird guide. There are many more. Visit your local bookstore or check the internet at bn.com or amazon.com, and you will find a wide assortment of field guides that will help you identify many different plants and animals.

Gallinule – Gallinules are birds that are shaped something like a chicken but live, feed and nest near water, especially in the southeastern part of the United States. The most likely gallinule that we will see when looking for them is the common gallinule. While it isn't very colorful, a relative, the purple gallinule, is quite beautiful.

Garter Snake – Garter snakes are rather medium-sized snakes that have stripes on their body. They are non-poisonous and generally feed on lizards, small mice and other small animals. There are many species with different markings on their body, and their appearance is something like another more slender snake called a ribbon snake.

Habitat – Habitats are certain types of areas that are distinct in one way or another, each habitat having its own types of plants and animals. Grasslands, pine woods, hardwood forests, wetlands and swamps are examples.

Hawk – Hawks are predatory birds, often feeding on different small animals. There are many types, all of which can be distinguished by using a bird field guide. Perhaps you can see an occasional hawk sitting on a wire near your house.

Heron – Herons, like egrets, are wading birds, feeding on fish, frogs, insects, even small snakes, in and by the water. Some types that are seen in parts of the United States are the Tri-colored Heron, Great Blue Heron, Little Blue Heron, and the Green Heron. Each has its particular way of catching its prey.

Hydrophobic Hairs – Hydrophobic hairs are hairs on the bodies of animals that repel water. They usually serve a particular purpose for the animal that has them. For instance, certain spiders have hydrophobic hairs that enable them to go into water and live for a while in a bubble that acts as a gill-like structure for the exchange of gasses, or it may just hold oxygen that the spider can breathe. The bubble is formed because of two features. Water molecules (H_2O) have properties that create a surface tension. Surface tension is a tension on the surface of the water that allows some insects and spiders to walk upon it. Surface tension and the hydrophobic hairs of insects and spiders sometimes work together, enabling them to form a bubble to breathe with. By doing this, insects and spiders can sometimes escape predators or feed on other things that live in the water.

Ibis – An ibis is a type of bird with a very long, recurved bill. It uses its bill to probe the ground so that it can feed on insects and other creatures that are found in those places. There are different species of ibis, such as the white ibis and glossy ibis. One species, the scarlet ibis, is a bright reddish color.

Indigenous – Indigenous animals and plants are native to the area in which they are found. Animals and plants that have originated in other areas but have been introduced to a new area are referred to as exotic species.

Indian – The word Indian in North America is used for people who were here before anyone else got here. Before Columbus found the New World, only Indians (also called Native Americans) lived here. Since the time of European arrival, beginning in the early 1500s, the North American Indian populations have gotten smaller, and they are usually found on reservations.

Insect – An insect is an animal referred to as an arthropod. Arthropods have two characteristics: an external skeleton (an exoskeleton) and jointed legs. There are many types, such as, insects, spiders, ticks, mites, crabs, lobsters, crayfish, millipedes, centipedes and many others. Insects represent a particular type of arthropod that has six legs and three body regions, the head, thorax, and abdomen. Some insects also have wings, but many do not.

Integument – An integument is the covering over an animal. Our integument is our skin, and it often has hairs sticking out of it. The integument or reptiles is a scaly skin. The integument of a bird is skin that has feathers sticking out of it. The integument of an insect or other type of arthropod is an exoskeleton.

Ladybird Beetle – A ladybird beetle is a type of beetle (an insect) that has an adult form with a round body and some form of pattern on its first pair of wings (its elytra). There are many species that are predaceous, preying upon other insects that they can find. They are often thought as beneficial to humans because they feed upon insects that harm our plants, such as aphids.

King Snake – There are many types of snakes in the world. A kingsnake is one type that often feeds on other snakes, as well as birds, bird eggs, rodents and many other small animals. There are many types. For instance, you may find one called the speckled king snake in and around Louisiana, another called the Florida king snake in parts of Florida, the Common King Snake in the eastern states, or the California King Snake in California. Some types of king snakes are quite beautiful, with rings of red, black and yellow on their body. All king snakes, of course, are harmless.

Migration – The term migration signifies a movement of animals from one place to another within its range, with a return trip back to the original spot. Monarch butterflies and numerous bird species are examples of migrating animals. Migration is most often associated with seasonal changes, movements in the northern hemisphere occurring toward the south in the Fall and toward the north during the Spring.

Mocking Bird – A black, gray and white bird with white wing patches and white sides along the tail. It is common and conspicuous in suburban habitats and fields. It is a bird that is often seen sitting upon light poles and heard singing in neighborhoods. It is especially territorial during the spring and summer months when it is nesting. Its songs are quite varied but are often complex phrases of melodies that are repeated two to six times.

Nocturnal – A term that means active at night. Certain animals prefer to be active at night, and they generally feed on other creatures that are active at the same time. *Diurnal* creatures are active by day, and *crepuscular* creatures are active at dawn and dusk.

Owl – A group of birds that are generally nocturnal predators with a hooked bill, sharp talons and forward-facing eyes. There are many types, including the barn owl, long-eared owl, great horned owl, barred owl, saw-whet owl, snowy owl, burrowing owl, elf owl and screech owl. A field guide to birds will give you information about and pictures of the different species.

Painted Bunting – One of a group of very colorful small birds that are found in grassy fields and woodland edges. The painted bunting is a very colorful species that is especially secretive. It is found throughout the eastern, southern and central states and is a welcome migrant.

Population – A population of organisms is a group of individuals that all belong to a single species and are in a certain place. For instance, we can speak of a population of humans, a population of a certain species of ants, or a population of deer. Populations of different plants and animals make up a community.

Racer – A name applied to a group of slender, very fast-moving non-poisonous snakes. They have a nasty disposition if cornered and will readily bite if caught. However, they are harmless. There are several types in the United States, such as the blue racer and black racer.

Reptile – A group of animals that are characterized by the presence of scales on their body. The group includes snakes, lizards, crocodilians and turtles. Species of reptiles and their pictures may be found in various field guides. See *Field Guides* above to find the proper one for this purpose.

Robin – A robin is a migratory bird that is found in many parts of the United States. They are found during the summer months in the North and during the winter in the South. They are sometimes called the Robin Redbreast because males have a reddish breast, especially during the breeding season.

Salamander – Salamanders are amphibians, and thus are related to frogs and toads. They resemble lizards superficially, but their life cycles are quite different. Salamanders deposit their eggs in water, and the young live in an aquatic habitat, breathing with gills, just like the tadpoles of frogs and toads. When most salamanders complete their development, they lose their gills and breathe with lungs, just like we do. Lizards deposit their eggs on land. There are a few salamanders that never lose their gills, and the adults must remain in water their entire life.

Solitary Living – When we speak of solitary living in animal populations, we generally mean that they do not live in family groups. A mud dauber is a good example. The female mud dauber builds a mud nest, into which she places food items, such as caterpillars or spiders that she paralyzes with her sting. She deposits an egg in the chamber and closes it off with more mud. Her offspring hatch inside and feed upon the prey items she had stocked it with. She doesn't offer any additional care to her young. They grow up by themselves, and when they emerge as adult wasps, they live a solitary life and never see their parents. Social species, however, live together, and their mothers and siblings take care of them. Humans are regarded as a social species.

Sound Production by Insects – Insects often produce sounds that are used by them to communicate with other members of their species. Examples of sounds that we are familiar with are those produced by grasshoppers and cicadas. The mechanisms by which they produce sounds are varied. For example, long-horned grasshoppers (such as katydids) and crickets, rub their wings together, producing sounds that we often hear during the evenings on warm summer days. Short-horned grasshoppers rub their legs on the side of their wings. Cicada males have a chamber in their body that they vibrate air through to produce the loud noises we hear on a summer evening. Some wasps make a buzzing noise when they build their nests. Many insects produce sounds that we are not able to hear, but they are heard by other members of their species. They hear these sounds by various means, often including membranes and special hairs that vibrate in a fashion similar to how our eardrums function.

Sparrow – A sparrow is a type of song bird. There are a number of types of sparrows. The most common bird in the United States that is referred to as a sparrow is the English Sparrow, but its not native to the United States, and it is really a finch rather than a sparrow.

Squirrel – Squirrels are rodent-like animals that specialize in feeding mostly on nuts. There are a number of species, including the Eastern Gray Squirrel and several species of Fox Squirrels. An unusual squirrel is the flying squirrel which is found primarily in the Southeastern United States.

Swamp – A swamp is usually a body of water that flows like a river but very slowly. The water in a swamp is generally filled with tannins, chemicals that washed down from the trees that live in that type of habitat. Animals and plants that live in a swamp often do not live anywhere else. One type of tree that usually defines a swamp is a cypress tree.

Toad – A toad is an amphibian. Other types of amphibians are frogs, salamanders and newts. The life cycle of such an amphibian usually has eggs that are deposited in water, immatures that live in water and breathe through gills and an adult stage that has lost its gills and tail and lives on land. Toads, like frogs, are often heard during the warm months of the year, singing their distinctive calls. Some people can tell what species of frog or toad is calling because each species is different.

Vulture – Vultures are large birds that are scavengers. This generally means that they will eat anything that has died. Two species are often seen in the United States. The most common one is the black buzzard, which has a black, featherless head. Its wings are shaped in such a way that they must fly by both gliding and flapping. The other species, the Turkey Buzzard, has a reddish, featherless head, and its wings are longer, enabling it to glide more, and their flight often enables them to flap their wings less.

Water Snake – There are many types of water snakes, most of which are harmless. Some types are the banded water snakes, green water snake, yellow bellied water snake and many others. The cottonmouth moccasin is venomous but is restricted to only the southeastern part of the United States. Many people call water snakes moccasins because they cannot tell the difference between the venomous and harmless species. A good field guide to the snakes will help you tell the difference.

Whip-O-Will – Whip-0-Wills are birds that are active at night. They get their name by the song they sing during the summer months. Birds referred to as nighthawks belong to the same group. Other related species have gotten their name from a variation of the whip-o-will's song, such as the Poor-Wills-Widow. Listen for them at night.

Winged – Animals with true wings are most birds, bats and many insects. A true wing is a wing that flaps and helps the animal become airborne. Some animals have flaps or skin that enable them to glide but not fly. Some birds do not have wings capable of making them airborne, such as emus, ostriches and kiwis. Many insects do not have wings.

Photo by L. D. Hermann

About the Author

Dr.Hermann has authored, coauthored and edited over 20 books on various topics. He has had extensive training in writing, editing and publishing, holding such positions as newspaper journalist, photojournalist and newspaper editor, science correspondent, science journal editor, proofreader, and consultant. He has also authored nine book chapters on various topics and hundreds of articles for scientific journals, magazines, and newspapers. His most recent academic book is *Dominance and Aggression in Humans and Other Animals* (Elsevier, 2016).

As former Professor in the Division of Biological Sciences at the University of Georgia, Lecturer in the Department of Science Education, Science Fair Coordinator and Judge, he maintained an interest in working with teachers and young people and enjoyed bridging the gap between them and science. It was for this reason that he developed several courses for teachers and coauthored a book (*Classroom Activities with Insects*) to convey information about science to their students. He also developed and taught courses directed at non-science college majors to bring some degree of science to individuals who were not science-oriented.

While on the Board of Directors at Sandy Creek Nature Center in Athens, Georgia, he worked with both teachers and young people and has taken part in many panel discussions to determine what it is that causes children to lose interest in science as they get older.

Dr. Hermann is currently teaching biology at Florida SouthWestern State College in Ft. Myers, Florida, where he also functions as Science Fair Judge for schools within the region. In recent years, he has published both fiction and non-fiction book titles. He is a member of the Gulf Coast Writers Association and Florida Writers Association, as well as being a Florida Writers Association Representative for Southwest Florida.

www.ingramcontent.com/pod-product-compliance
Lightning Source LLC
Chambersburg PA
CBHW060256050426
42448CB00009B/1659